D1432464

SCULPTURE AT GOODWOOD

Dedicated to the commissioning,
promotion and sale of British
contemporary sculpture

www.sculpture.org.uk

British Contemporary Sculpture at Goodwood 1998-99

As we publish our fourth Sculpture at Goodwood book, and take stock of the last four years, we are truly amazed to find that over fifty new sculptures have been produced as a result of our commissioning process. The original vision that pieces would be sold around the world is being realised and thus Sculpture at Goodwood is truly promoting the strength of British contemporary sculpture around the world as the century ends.

This year we have commissioned and installed some eighteen new sculptures. It is wonderful for us to see our collaborative efforts taking shape in all their variety, and to see our dream become a reality.

Our educational objectives for the foundation have also progressed. Conversations between artists and critics, historians or architects continue to take place four times a year. These are recorded, and are broadcast the next day on our website, which now numbers over a thousand pages. With the sculptors' drawings and models collection growing,we are now in the position to launch them as a touring exhibition. This exhibition, named *A Labour of Love*, opened at Pallant House Gallery in September 1998, and is now available for other venues. A book on the drawings and models 1994-1998 is published concurrently with this volume.

We are grateful to Ann Elliott, who was our Head of Sculpture for three years until 1997 and who has been responsible for the writing of this book. She continues to advise us on curatorial matters while pursuing a freelance career in the arts. Our special thanks also to our volunteers without whom Sculpture at Goodwood could not carry out its many-sided activities. Tom Flynn has written the very interesting introductory article after his recent visit to Goodwood.

Wilfred and Jeannette Cass

Opposite: *Confessional* by Cathy de Monchaux (see page 58).

A Genealogy of Excellence

On my recent visit to Sculpture at Goodwood I came across a new work – *Land-Bin* by Andrew Sabin – being installed within a forest clearing. Into Sabin's elegant, bifurcated aluminium basket Martin Russell and William Jenkins, Goodwood's two technicians, were shovelling compacted leaves and other forest mulch. They paused to explain how eventually the accumulated strata of organic debris would fill the galvanised steel bin, thereby completing the work.

Sabin's *Land-Bin* functions as an apt visual metaphor for the broader Goodwood sculpture project, enacting as it does the symbiotic relationship between sculpture and place. Just as the forest cradles and contains the works selected for exhibition, so too does the forest become temporarily part of the work. This cross-pollination between the objects and their location – which in no way impinges upon the aesthetic autonomy of the pieces on show – is what has made Sculpture at Goodwood so successful and is what will surely guarantee it longevity.

It is eight years since Wilfred and Jeannette Cass took their first steps towards establishing a home for British contemporary sculpture at Hat Hill Copse on the Goodwood estate. Now that the project has consolidated and matured, the present time seems an ideal moment to step back and assess the significance of their achievement.

Establishing an open-air exhibition space is a precarious venture even for the seasoned professional curator, requiring energy, determination and resourcefulness, to say nothing of a considerable financial outlay. However, all these practical requirements are as nothing without spadefuls of self-belief and, above all, an unshakeable faith in the worth of British contemporary sculpture. It has been a combination of all these qualities which has made Goodwood such a dynamic facilitator of new work. In its fourth anniversary year, Goodwood continues to draw global attention to the importance of British sculpture and continues to incubate innovative sculptural projects. The vista is continually shifting, however, as sculptures come and go. Nevertheless, within the changing landscape is a seam of continuity, a genealogy of creative excellence which has won British sculptors an enviable international reputation and which has visitors returning again and again. Each year around a third of the works move on to new homes, thereby making way for new commissions and fresh opportunities. This rhythmic rotation testifies both to the strong international demand for British work, and to the consistent quality of the pieces being produced to meet that demand.

It is a lamentable reflection of the paucity of public funding that it took a private initiative to illuminate the full extent of British sculptural talent, and today it remains hard to believe that Hat Hill Copse is still the only place where one can experience together a range of first-rate, large-scale work by the likes of Anthony Caro, Tony Cragg, Bill Woodrow, David Nash, William Turnbull, Bernard Meadows, Kenneth Armitage and Lynn Chadwick, as well as work by younger artists such as Andy Goldsworthy, David Mach, Shirazeh Houshiary, Nicola Hicks, Vong Phaophanit and Dhruva Mistry, to name but a small sample.

Such a list offers an indication of the enthusiasm with which the Goodwood initiative is being embraced by contemporary artists and is in itself good enough reason to make a visit. What is more, to locate anything up to forty works within the 20-acre forest while maintaining the integrity of each individual piece is no mean achievement. Success in this regard requires a keen understanding of how sculpture interacts with the *genius loci*.

A flexible, open-ended approach to commissioning offers artists the freedom to explore personal visions, to experiment with expanded scale, or to engage with unfamiliar materials – all issues that might be foreclosed by more restricting sculptural contracts. It is estimated that in ten years' time there will be around 130 works out in the world which would not otherwise have been realised, giving a sense of the vitality of British contemporary sculpture and the extent to which it has responded to this particular stimulus. This does not take into account the independent commissions that have come to many of the sculptors as a consequence of having shown here, nor the exhibitions that have been forthcoming. One notable instance was Bill Woodrow's 1996 exhibition at the Tate Gallery which followed from a tour of Goodwood by the Tate's guides where they encountered some of his recent work.

Those who have not yet made a visit to Hat Hill Copse might assume that the enterprise exists solely to market British sculpture to the curators of wealthy international collections. While that aspect is of obvious importance, and has proved unexpectedly fruitful, the Goodwood project also functions to awaken an appreciation of sculpture in the casual visitor. Among the more telling testimonials are those from organisers of school trips who relate the therapeutic effect which the open-air sculpture seems to exert on even the most unruly of pupils. Such apparently light-hearted feedback should be taken seriously, for it testifies to the nourishing power of art on the sensibilities of children, who may one day assume responsibility for these environments or who may, as a consequence of their visit, be inspired to become artists themselves. Sculpture at Goodwood continues to provide a stimulating learning environment for visitors of all ages and backgrounds.

This year, 1998, sees yet another influx of new sculpture. Visitors will turn a corner and be surprised by Nicola Hicks's *Recovered Memory*, an unsettlingly posed encounter between a totemic, lupine figure and a diminutive young girl who together lock glances in a silent dialogue of mutual fascination. Cast in bronze from an original modelled in Hicks's favoured medium of plaster and straw (as though from the forest's own consitituent elements), *Recovered Memory* gains much of its power from the open-air location. Forests are the traditional *mise en scène* of fairy tale and legend, but this group also makes oblique references to a more disturbing cultural archive of child abuse. The tension between these two conflicting narratives invests the piece with a peculiar resonance.

The work of 1998 Turner Prize nominee Cathy de Monchaux is rarely encountered in the open air. *Confessional*, a Gothicky, gazebo-like structure standing in its own sheltered glade, is her first piece for Goodwood and transposes her deeply personal juxtapositions of soft and hard materials into architectonic dimensions. De Monchaux's *Confessional* – its interior reassuringly sheathed in suede while bristling with corten steel spikes – reminds us that the luxury of repentance is also a launch-pad to further transgressions.

William Furlong's new work, *Walls of Sound*, is the first audible sculpture to enter Hat Hill Copse. A corridor of parallel stainless steel walls has been installed with amplified recordings of the chirping, rustle and scrape of the surrounding region's flora and fauna – the sound-track of the countryside obligingly condensed for the displaced urban *flâneur*. Appropriately, Furlong's sound piece now occupies the space vacated by Vong Phaophanit's recently departed electronic *Azure Neon Body* which had been the first work to introduce artificial light into the forest.

However, it is not only the recently installed works which demand attention today, for many of the pieces which have been on site for a season or more still seem fresh and challenging. None more so than William Tucker's bronze *Frenhofer* of 1997, which continues to assert its powerful presence, as though some deep geological seam had erupted from beneath the forest floor. This chthonic lump remains the most insistently sculptural object at Goodwood, demanding continuous reappraisal and endorsing Donald Kuspit's recent remark that: 'It is the inexplicable expressivity of matter in Tucker's recent works that bespeaks what is most fundamental to the body, reaching a substratum of emotional truth.' Perhaps more than any other work, *Frenhofer* tends to generate passionate aesthetic debate among visitors, and because of this it will be sorely missed when it departs.

Erratic outcrops of rocky bronze; bodies of azure neon light; granite catamarans on granite waves; towers of discovery; pillars of salt; walls of sound; forest, earth and sky - the poetic inventory which began at Sculpture at Goodwood in 1994 continues to expand. This year William Pye irrigates the atmosphere with a new work entitled Miss *Prism,* a nine-foot stainless steel monolith whose concealed electric motor sends a continuous veil of water shimmering down its sides, only to climb invisibly back to its summit. You will see the trees refracted in abstract through that stream of falling water and you may also catch a glimpse of why Sculpture at Goodwood works.

Tom Flynn
Henry Moore Research Fellow
University of Sussex

Taking the Bait

In establishing Sculpture at Goodwood, Wilfred and Jeannette Cass set themselves high standards and clearly defined goals. They were driven by a desire for quality and the need for marketing innovation. Their passion for British contemporary sculpture led them forward. During the first four years they have followed their chosen path, and change occurs in response to the needs of an evolving project. In the early days before opening the grounds to the public their concerns were to organise the woodland into proper areas to receive sculptures, to engage the interest of artists of sufficient calibre, and to convince everyone of the seriousness of their intent. A substantial financial commitment was needed to realise their vision, and Wilfred and Jeannette Cass have given many millions of pounds to the creation of new sculptures and to establishing an exceptional venue and promotional facility. Their continuing investment now and beyond their own lifetimes will secure long-term support for British sculpture.

There can be no doubt that the confidence in Sculpture at Goodwood evinced by Sir Anthony Caro spread to other members of Britain's artistic community. His loan of *The Tower of Discovery* 1991, which looked magnificent on the southern perimeter of the grounds in the first years, encouraged many other artists to become involved.

Established art organisations and gallery owners with the common aim of nurturing the work of British sculptors are beginning to see how they are able to work together with Sculpture at Goodwood. The Henry Moore Sculpture Trust initiated work on some of the sculptures that have been installed at Goodwood: Sir Anthony Caro's *Goodwood Steps* 1994-96, William Tucker's *Frenhofer* 1997 and Tony Cragg's *Pillars of Salt* 1998.

As Sculpture at Goodwood is a non-profit making organisation it was sculpture and to promote that work, filling the gap between the artist and his maquette and the potential collector. Spin-offs to the activity are also important. These include a wonderful environment to show sculptures to the best advantage, a commitment to new technologies which spread information about those sculptures with immense speed and skill throughout the world, an educational facility, and a conduit for artists to market their work internationally.

Early experiments with digital imaging of artists' works have developed in sophistication through Sculpture at Goodwood's first four years. The Internet site is one of the most exciting and innovative for the visual arts world wide. Sculptures which have been at Goodwood since the beginning are recorded and archived on the site, and live web-casts of conversations between artists and critics, art historians, curators or architects are now a regular feature. It is a compelling site to browse, and weekly visits are now in the region of eight hundred to one thousand. As an educational and outreach facility www.sculpture.org.uk is extremely effective.

Since Sculpture at Goodwood first opened an annual guide book has been published. In seeking a different format for a publication on sculpture, the first book evolved from an idea to produce a series of 'prompt ' cards on the sculptures and the artists for the volunteer guides. These were very well received by the guides, so the size remained the same and the 'cards' became the bound volume. Many visitors use the book whilst walking in the grounds, some use it for later reference. As more are published they build a history of British sculpture as seen through the commissions at Sculpture at Goodwood. The books also play a part in reminding potential collectors of the fact that it is possible for them to purchase monumental works of art which, before Sculpture at Goodwood, they would have commissioned as an act of faith. The books are Sculpture at Goodwood's first branch of outreach, a promotional and marketing tool, reaching out to collectors, to artists, to arts specialists and to the general public. More branches have evolved and grown through the passage of time and through the search for different avenues of contact and enquiry.

Finding the best form of outreach activity for Sculpture at Goodwood has taken time. Potential collaborators were apprehensive of this new project, although enthusiastic associations were formed with South East Arts and with West Sussex County Council. Some good educational projects flourished and sculptures were commissioned through local authority developments in Shoreham, in Crawley and with South East Water at the Ardingly Reservoir, all of which are continuing.

Developing new partnerships to commission sculpture and to place it in the public domain has this year resulted in a fruitful collaboration between the Royal Society of Arts and Sculpture at Goodwood. The empty plinth in Trafalgar Square has long been a subject of debate, and the plan to place newly commissioned sculptures there, each for a period of around one year, is beginning to take shape. Sculptures by Mark Wallinger, Rachel Whiteread and Bill Woodrow will successively inhabit the plinth before being shown at Sculpture at Goodwood from where they will be sold. In financing and managing the project, Sculpture at Goodwood takes its ethos into the centre of London. It is important to point out that this project is at an early stage and planning permission, amongst other permissions, has yet to be granted.

Chichester Institute of Higher Education, which is part of Portsmouth University, has participated in a new research project with Sculpture at Goodwood. It became very clear to Wilfred Cass in his discussions with artists that a survey and annotated index of sculptors' materials and technologies available to artists would be very useful. The research is in progress and the results will be published through Goodwood's Internet site so that artists from all over the world may benefit.

Others have embraced Goodwood's example in different ways. Visits to Sculpture at Goodwood by Councillors and Officers from the Royal Borough of Kensington and Chelsea inspired them to take forward their plans for a millennium sculpture exhibition in Holland Park. Reviving a long tradition of sculpture exhibitions in the park organised from the fifties to the seventies by the former GLC, this will run from March 2000 to March 2001.

Aspects of Goodwood's practice have been seized upon by others and emulated, in particular the core activity of helping artists to realise works which they might not otherwise be be able to achieve. Mile End Park Partnership saw this method of working as a possibility for their newly developing Artspark, and the park will eventually have an area where sculptures will be shown regularly on a similar basis.

A recent initiative of the British High Commission and the British Council in Canada is to show new sculptures by British artists in Ottawa, as part of a year-long festival of British culture. The British High Commission is a large building in the city centre, and works by Laura Ford and Paul Neagu, helped originally by Sculpture at Goodwood, and a new carving by Peter Randall-Page will be installed there in the early autumn of 1998.

A sign that Sculpture at Goodwood is beginning to exert its own influence may be seen from the number of artists and designers who have received commissions through their work having been seen in the grounds. Collectors and people commissioning new pieces have found inspiration in the work and in the setting Sculpture at Goodwood provides. There have also been many enquiries and visits from people wanting to start their own sculpture gardens or trails, from places as far flung as America, Australia, Italy, New Zealand and Switzerland as well as in Britain.

Last summer saw the first Sculpture at Goodwood Collectors' Day. The success of the day was underlined by many subsequent expressions of interest in the sculptures, purchases and favourable press commentary. This led to the decision to hold similar events once every two years. The next will be held in June 1999.

There are at least eighteen new monumental sculptures in the process of being realised for Sculpture at Goodwood which will grace the grounds through next season. More work will be undertaken on modifying the maturing woodland to keep abreast of growth and decay in the plant population, ensuring that there will always be proper, discrete places for the sculptures. These activities set the scene, but without the thoughtful commitment of the sculptors themselves none of this would be possible, as it is their new work which remains central to Sculpture at Goodwood.

Ann Elliott

Sir Anthony Caro
Goodwood Steps (Spirals) 1994-96
steel, L 32 m
Enabled by the Henry Moore Sculpture Trust and Sculpture at Goodwood

'*Goodwood Steps* started from a work that I made indoors in Halifax, Yorkshire, and whilst working on this piece I realised that it would be quite different from the Halifax work, which was a sculpture inside a room with a stone floor. Although it was an open form, it was very enclosed within the room. *Goodwood Steps* is a sculpture against a landscape. You can get away from it, see it whole, look at it from above, and you are conscious of the view of the countryside through it and the big sky. However, the sculpture still relates intimately to the viewer. Walking along its length and under the steps one gets a kind of physical experience - something like the way the viewer experienced *The Tower of Discovery* which stood at Sculpture at Goodwood for three years.

'I have been fascinated by the project because it's so architectural. Because of this the piece seems to bear a different relation to us and to the environment from what we normally expect of sculpture. The repetition and mechanical elements are a counterpoint to the grand view of the downs - not as in the work of Moore, which was often a reminder of the landscape, but as a contrast to it, much in the way that the mechanical shape of a windmill brings a human dimension to the land.'

This statement was made by Anthony Caro at Goodwood whilst he was working on the sculpture.

SCULPTURE

Nigel Ellis

Mindfulness of Breathing 1998
steel, painted, H 300 cm, edition 1/3
Enabled by Sculpture at Goodwood

This is an embracing sculpture of deceptive simplicity, which focuses the attention of the viewer through fundamental forms. Two wedge-shaped elements present their square faces to one another. Each face bears a circle, convex in one and concave in the other. There is enough space for the viewer to move between them. The outer faces similarly contain convex and concave circular forms, suggesting that the related parts could go on for ever in a continuous line. These basically described characteristics which are perceived and readily understood in the literal sense present the viewer with a direct experience to question. What else is convex or concave? What does the title give us? How do these forms work as a metaphor for someone else's ideas? In this case, *Mindfulness of Breathing* is a Buddhist meditation, an exercise concentrating the mind through awareness of regular breaths. The facing concave and convex forms give us inward and outward direction, a parallel for inward and outward breaths. They are also positive and negative, much as a mould in the making of sculpture is a negative form which gives shape to the 'positive' sculpture. In painting the textured surface of the sculpture white, Nigel Ellis denies the steel its material quality. The large sweeping areas take the light according to the weather conditions, the season or the time of day. Sometimes the concave or convex motifs are softly contoured by the light, at other times they are defined starkly.

As you walk through the space defined by the elemental forms of square, circle and triangle, the scale contains you, and your awareness - which might well be the real subject of this sculpture - completes the physical experience. In contemplating this piece, empty your mind, listen to your own calm breathing, and look for the hidden meanings that *Mindfulness of Breathing* can convey.

Steven Gregory
The Two of Us 1997-98
bronze, H 350 cm, edition 1/3
Enabled by Sculpture at Goodwood

'Would you care to dance, Mrs Hippo?' 'Certainly, sir!' she said. Round and round they went, their fat blubbery forms appearing to have the lightness of thistledown as they spun across the the ballroom floor. Occasionally the rattle of a teacup punctuated the Valse des Fleurs. Other couples, shuffling or treading on each other's feet, looked in awe at the pair, marvelling at their dimension as well as the precision of their movement. Totally at one, they danced the afternoon away. The medium of music and the location of the Mecca dance hall, every Tuesday and Thursday afternoon, from three until five-thirty, gave escape to this couple who, in their everyday lives, would lumber for the bus and strain to enter the Underground train before the door closed.

In this sculpture Steven Gregory has given lightness to volume, and in so doing has given a lie to the density and weight of bronze. If we look at this two-piece sculpture in terms of composition, rhythm, volume, mass, texture and colour it works, formally. A harmonious whole, the composition satisfies from every point of view. Form is accentuated by texture, careful colouring and tonal rendering of the patina. The open flowers of the lips are sensual whilst conveying a notion of vacuousness and mystery. The intimate touch of this pair appears tentative and polite, their toes enjoying the closest contact. What are these creatures? They are the product of Gregory's imagination, and revealed themselves first in a drawing which came, he thinks, but cannot be sure, from his fascination with a television wildlife programme about the hippopotamus. These lumbering, ungainly creatures on land took on qualities of utmost grace when in water. As an idea for a sculpture, this notion would work in abstract form. Steven Gregory, however, has chosen to present his sculptural ideas in a figurative mode whilst imbuing them with qualities of humour and ridicule.

Glynn Williams
Gateway of Hands 1992
bronze, H 335 cm, edition 1/3
Enabled by Sculpture at Goodwood

This is Glynn Williams's largest sculpture to date, of which there are two casts in bronze. This, the original, welcomes visitors to Sculpture at Goodwood.

The piece is typical of Williams's work, demonstrating his unique blend of figuration and abstraction. He first employed the notion of slicing into naturalistic forms and shifting the pieces into new relationships in *Portrait with Flowers* 1990-91, which was shown at Sculpture at Goodwood during the first season. The dynamism which he found this method of working gave to the forms can be seen in the hands, which from the front look quite realistic, but from behind take on a curious ambiguity. With the hands, the implied movement of opening the palm in a gesture of welcome is underlined by the centre sections of each hand being sliced and swivelled, out in one, slightly inward in the other; pushed forward in one and slightly back in the other. The way in which the hands interact is also curious. Having been parted in the gesture of greeting, they are sited as two separate elements, but the composition remains as one, largely through the continuation of strong diagonals in each which are readily linked by the eye.

Such compositional devices were used by the cubists in their quest for a better understanding of form. In Picasso's *Glass of Absinthe*, he moved portions of the glass and its contents into new relationships to give a whole view: an entire experience of seeing round and within the form. So it is with these hands.

The hands are a self-portrait, undeniably those of their maker.

Iain Edwards
Reinventing the Wheel 1998
Wood, metal, painted, various dimensions
The Artist

An innate respect for craftsmanship and the need to make things well has informed Iain Edwards's sculptural vocabulary. Over the last five or six years he has travelled extensively, and his sculptures carry hints of diverse memories - a New York skyscraper, a tram in Amsterdam, a Roman temple, or southern Indian processional carts, shown several years ago at the Whitechapel Art Gallery. The artist's task was to make sense of his exposure to much visual stimulus, and Edwards brought these things to his work as a way of developing a formal language whilst working within the limitations of wood and steel sheeting used in combination.

In the first of these compositions the wheel form is still largely the subject, but it is pushed towards being something different, a container and a lid. The idea of giving land-based forms the uncertain support of wheels makes light of objects that are intrinsically heavy. Movement is implied, but not possible. These wheels are fixed; the artist remains in control.

Gradually Edwards has introduced colour into his sculptures. He is uneasy about colour, but it works well where he uses it to draw our eye to parts of the sculpture that we may overlook. He also uses colour to define limits, linking a roof with wheels, or to demonstrate other boundaries by showing a way and then blocking it. The colours resonate although they are low-key. Worked into the wood or metal with wire wool, they become part of the base material, particularly when waxed to a luminous satin finish.

Ian Hamilton Finlay

The World Has Been Empty Since the Romans 1985
Bath stone, steel chain, L 735 cm
Victoria Miro, London

These slabs of stone, resembling fragments from a Roman archaeological site, with their carefully inscribed words in classical letter-form, are a very bleak statement. Made in collaboration with a stone mason, the poem sets up trails of thoughts about European culture. But is this rhetoric? Is it a metaphor? Finlay proposes the right sentiment through the most appropriate medium, and we believe that at Hat Hill, close to evidence of Roman occupation, the sculpture has found its most fitting place.

The possibility that such fragments may have fallen from the inscribed architrave of a Roman temple is suggested by the way in which Finlay has displayed them. Reassembled, like portions of a jigsaw, the stones are hung in line, not only for the message to be read, but to give museological overtones which may also underline the philosophical content of the work.

THE·WORLD·HAS·BEEN·EMPTY·SINCE·THE·ROMAN

Lynn Chadwick
Stranger III 1959 (cast 1996)
bronze, L 264 cm, edition 4/4
Enabled by Sculpture at Goodwood

One of only a handful of public commissions undertaken by Chadwick, *Stranger III*, originally commissioned by the Air League of the British Empire, gave him an opportunity to work on a monumental scale. This sculpture was to commemorate the double crossing of the Atlantic by the Airship R 34 in July 1919, and was to be placed outside the Long Haul Terminal at Heathrow Airport.

The architect of the terminal, Frederick Gibberd, the Royal Fine Art Commission, the Minister of Transport, Harold Watkinson, and the Committee of the Air League were all enthusiastic about the sculpture. However, in 1958 an opposing committee led by Lord Brabazon of Tara, who called the sculpture a 'diseased Haddock', with the Guild of Air Pilots and Aviators behind him, forced the Air League to withdraw the commission. Lynn Chadwick made one cast in 1959 which has since been destroyed. Of the declared edition of four, one is sited publicly in Spoleto, Italy, another is at Colby College, Bixler Art and Music Center in Maine and a third in Belgium. Sculpture at Goodwood has completed the edition with this cast made at Pangolin Editions in Gloucestershire, from a moulding taken from the piece in Belgium.

The winged figure is a development from the maquette, *Stranger II* 1958. The maquette shows two figures merging with the heads looking both to the left and right, symbolising the double transatlantic journey, with spread symmetrical wings. In the final figure Chadwick has foreshortened one wing and tapered the other, whilst maintaining a compositional balance.

Dhruva Mistry
The Object 1995-97
stainless steel, H 400 cm, edition 1/3
Enabled by Sculpture at Goodwood

In 1987 Dhruva Mistry made a number of medallions within which he used images of objects such as a chair which he then developed in two different ways, the object as a representation of human presence and as a more organic thing evolving towards human form. This sculpture is a further development, woven with other ideas explored as early as 1976 in works combining the human figure with cubes, which evolved towards the physical content becoming entirely geometrical. Here, the subject is the object, and Mistry plays with that area between the onlooker and the object with the intention of making the onlooker's perception become the content. *The Object* is perceived by looking at it, looking into it, looking round it and looking through it.

The overall quality of the piece is well defined in terms of planes, forms and cut-outs. The planes are meant to work architecturally, and are here combined with an interest in crystalline forms which may be seen through - the roof being a crystal shape which might be read either as a crystal or a roof. The entrance is an invitation into the object/palace/castle/dream-castle where there are signs of welcome, but physical entry is impossible. Any idea of reality is constantly confounded. As the viewer looks at one side of the sculpture expectations are set up, only to be dashed as he/she moves around it.

Dhruva Mistry is very clear about his play on perception. In this sculpture the play on meaning and on language, almost a tease, is taken full distance, with the material quality of *The Object* having equal physical and intellectual weight. Stainless steel, sanded to a mellow silvery surface is, for Mistry, the perfect medium through which to deliver this piece. Treated in this way, steel has an ambiguity that distances itself from the physicality of stone.

Keir Smith
Stefano 1997
bronze, H 518 cm
Enabled by Sculpture at Goodwood

St Sigismondo, a Renaissance church in Cremona, provided Keir Smith with the point of departure in developing his ideas for this sculpture. Since he has had a long and academic interest in the art of the Renaissance throughout his career, it may seem surprising that this passion has not surfaced before in Smith's work. This dormant force was unleashed when he made his first visit to Italy in 1989, and on a typically hot and dusty August afternoon came across the church. The cool, dark interior, with light from the high rose window in the west wall pouring into the chapel of Saints Caterina and Cecilia on the northern side of the church, had a significant impact on Smith, and has directly informed the palpable nature of the sculpture. This experience coincided with a period of continual drawing, which from time to time Smith has pursued to the exclusion of working in three dimensions. Drawing in such a concentrated manner, searching for form and content which he could bring together in his sculpture, resulted in *The Cremona Wilderness*, a series of works in watercolour and pencil on paper depicting objects and buildings in barren rocky landscapes.

Stefano emerged from the series, together with another sculpture, *The Tomb of Francesco*, on which Keir Smith has worked concurrently. St Stephen was stoned to death for blasphemy, and the pile of stones viewed beyond the portion of the church, together with the single rock on the altar piece of the sculpture, have become icons for the martyr. The sculpture represents a section through the church of St Sigismondo with its walls dissolved to reveal the cairn of golden stones and the distant landscape. Absorbing the landscape into the sculpture in this way was a theme of Smith's earlier work, which was made almost entirely to commission and in response to particular sites. Here the landscape is incidental, but acknowledged.

John Davies
Head 1997
bronze, H 210 cm, edition 1/2
Enabled by Sculpture at Goodwood

In his early sculpture John Davies used a room or exhibition gallery as a theatre, devising spaces to see how individually made figures worked together, moving them around as an abstract sculptor might move stones or wood to form different relationships. Gesture was important and remains so today, particularly in his drawings, as does the element of story telling. Davies makes small models or maquettes and life-sized human figures which relate in tension and narrative, and has now added exceptionally large heads to his repertoire. For him these new extremes of scale provide opportunities to explore how the human figure may be perceived and how we can relate to it differently. The minute figures with their intense detail endow the viewer with authority. The large heads, with no less detail in their surface, reduce the viewer to the stature of a child, where a hand in relation to a face is tiny and the surface appears to be awesome.

John Davies has spent the last four years working on a group of large heads in an attempt to get as near as possible to his subject. Two or three of these massive heads, placed so close together that you have to squeeze between them would give the sensation of being in a crowd or they might be like ancient standing stones or massive rocks which were also faces. These heads pose questions for the viewer about the relevance of making figures in the late twentieth century, about the role of figurative sculpture at this time, and about the possibility of knowing ourselves. Sculpture, in John Davies's opinion, may become a talisman for the age in which it was made. Looking back at Giotto, for example, the humanity in his groups of figures, their gesture, iconography and sculptural form are as relevant now as they were five hundred years ago. They became a talisman of the early Renaissance, and possibly these heads may become ours for the end of the twentieth century.

Maggie Cullen
Untitled I 1997
acrylic, sanded, D 145 cm
The Artist

Untitled I is one of a series of three sculptures in which Maggie Cullen strove to devise a technology to meet an aesthetic she required of her chosen material. The process became a two-year project. She writes, 'The sculpture is made from acrylic sheet which has been sanded to create a surface of cuts which attract the surrounding light and radiate it back to the viewer. This diffusion of light and subsequent appearance of weightlessness attracted me to the material.' Her inspiration for the sculptures, she claims, ' . . . came from a magical afternoon spent in the Alhambra, Granada in 1990,' and was the first time she had attempted to convey 'the emotional impact of a defining moment; a moment of aesthetic intensity and joy.'

The sculptures marked a departure from her previous work in which Cullen used found and cast objects. Her interest in objects which were functional as well as having beauty in their form and design influenced her work more directly than it does now. Her early training as a ceramicist has also informed her work and she developed a keen sense of form and an eye for the openings that pots naturally have. The outline of *Untitled I* may be seen as that of a container although the series of acrylic sheets which give rhythm to the sculpture defy that notion in the literal sense. They may be read as strata through the form, even though the original shape would have been defined by space within a skin. She writes, 'I am often reminded of Heidegger's parable of the jug where it is the void within and not the material which determines the form of the vessel.'

The intensity of light that Cullen has achieved in this sculpture serves to disguise certain aspects of its construction, which adds a sense of mystery to the undeniable beauty of the object.

Tony Cragg
The Spill 1987
bronze, L 300 cm
Private loan

On leaving school and before enrolling at Wimbledon College of Art, Tony Cragg worked as a laboratory assistant in Liverpool. The experience has emerged again and again in his work through images of laboratory vessels which he interprets variously as literal enlargements, as forms which indicate different kinds of evolution, or as shapes which are altered through his intervention. In *Spill* he has taken as his subject a vessel for heating liquid. Clearly, the vessel has fallen over as it has no base. It is the kind of container that should be held in a metal collar above a Bunsen burner in order that the contents may be heated. The liquid inside this particular container has spilt, the container lies on its side and the contents stream out (at Goodwood into the path of the passing visitor.) A metaphor for the molten quality of bronze is certainly apparent here, as it is a possible interpretation of the subject and is integral to the object.

Cragg's works are full of play on certain kinds of reality, and this work is no exception. The sculpture looks as the title insists it should, but there is much more to delve into. In terms of dimension, this is is a simple enlargement, for the glass container in the laboratory would have been a fraction of the size. But there is more to think about. How differently do we perceive this vessel when it is presented in another medium? Why is there a spill? Who was responsible? What would the liquid have been? The scenarios are endless, but all come from this simple proposition.

Tony Cragg pushes forward the possibilities for sculpture more than many of his contemporaries, and *Spill* is a prime example of this achievement.

Nicola Hicks
Recovered Memory 1996-97
bronze, H 22 cm, edition 2/6
Enabled by Sculpture at Goodwood

We know well from the children's tale of Little Red Riding Hood that the Wolf assumes the identity of Grandmother by dressing in her clothes. This late twentieth-century wolf in the Sussex woodland looks meek and mild in a frock, and because of the fairy story we can safely suppose that the wolf's gender is male. The polite encounter between disguised male adult and female child and the courtesy of their slight curtsies leads us to consider the possibility of sinister intent on the one hand and innocence with trust on the other. Horror experienced at second hand through bedtime stories in the safety of the nursery can unfortunately be a reality today.

In his catalogue essay to Nicola Hicks's exhibition, *Furtive Imagination*, held at the Whitworth Art Gallery, Manchester, in 1997, Michael Simpson writes: 'In today's society we have become uncomfortably conscious of the power adults can have physically, emotionally and sexually over children . . . Tens of thousands of adults throughout the world are being encouraged by the psychoanalysts to "recover" memories stored away beneath layers of denial.' The encounter between child and adult in this sculpture suggests that memory may be recovered through simply acknowledging the traditional tale, and on a more complex level may reveal truths about ourselves.

The original sculpture from which this bronze version is cast was modelled in plaster and straw built on a wire framework. The straw gives texture and bulk to the plaster and Hicks allows the stalks to be revealed in some portions of the figures. The back of the child's dress and the wolf's head are enlivened by the the way in which the straw springs free.

Andy Goldsworthy
Herd of Arches 1994
sandstone and slate, L 1500 cm (approx)
Michael Hue-Williams, London

The quarry at Gatelawbridge in Dumfriesshire was the site of a work which is illustrated in *Stone* by Andy Goldsworthy (Viking/Penguin Books, 1994) under the inscription:

> Out of the quarry
> seven arches
> made over two days
> no failures
> one almost fell -
> slipped down the face of a rock
> as I removed supporting stones

This was the first manifestation of the sandstone arches, made entirely in the spirit of Goldsworthy's practice of using materials in their place of origin. The stone from this quarry was used in the construction of major eighteenth- and nineteenth-century buildings which make up much of Glasgow, the distinct pink colour lending warmth to the northern townscape.

This notion of movement found its way into *Herd of Arches*, a group which seems to have wandered in search of a new location. Sited by Andy Goldsworthy and Joe Smith at Hat Hill Copse, the *Arches* are placed along a pathway winding between fairly dense trees, against a dark green ground-cover of ivy. Here the colour contrast between the red stone and the green ground lends a strong dynamic to the piece, which first emerged against its own colour in the rough waste ground of the quarry.

David Mach
The Garden Urn 1996
galvanised wire coat hangers, H 250 cm
Enabled by Sculpture at Goodwood

David Mach employs no end of curious and unrelated materials and man-made objects in his sculpture. From piles of unused newspapers and magazines he has fashioned full-scale classical columns; from rubber tyres, submarines and Greek temples; from match heads, the most colourful portraits, and from burnt match heads, sombre ones. It is from the match heads that a series of portraits using wire coat hangers emerged. The sitter's face was modelled, and the contours described with closely assembled rows of hangers, the hooks providing a shimmering aura around the head.

This *Garden Urn* came about because David Mach was interested in the over-decorated, reproduction garden urns that can be found in garden centres. Given Mach's long fascination with kitsch items this was not unusual, but the twist in the tale came when Sculpture at Goodwood asked him for one of his wire coat hanger garden urns. He had not made one, but thought this to be a reasonable idea for a sculpture. We found that the gardens of Biddulph Grange, a National Trust property in Staffordshire, had the ideal sugar-bowl urn. With the help of the head gardener, Bill Maleclei, photographs were taken and the shape and scale approved by Mach. The National Trust's Mercia Regional Office gave permission for Mach's assistant, Philip Stroud, to take a copy of the urn, which he made in fibreglass. The fibreglass version is displayed tipped over, spilling fruits onto the ground, opulent and extravagant. The coat hangers were laboriously assembled by Adrian Moakes at his workshops in Manchester. The result is a sculpture of enormous humour and curious beauty, resplendent in a sylvan setting, which cocks a snook at our preconceptions and desires for the status that such objects are supposed to imply.

William Furlong
Walls of Sound 1998
stainless steel, L 1220 cm, edition 1/3
Enabled by Sculpture at Goodwood

As a child in a Catholic primary school, William Furlong remembers one of the sisters asking the class to close their eyes and to listen very carefully. The sounds that he heard surprised him, and it became clear to him that we never, or hardly ever, live in complete silence. There is always some ambient sound - someone breathing, distant traffic, bird song, an occasional cough or a dog barking. This example is offered, not to suggest that Furlong immediately became an artist who uses sound as part of his repertoire, but to describe an experience that remained with him and which is relevant to his current practice as an artist.

Walls of Sound is a sculpture not only for the visual, but also for the aural sense. William Furlong uses stainless steel, digital discs and amplifiers as well as the sounds that he records and alters in many different ways so that they are right for the work, much as a painter might mix pigments on his palette. In this case the recordings were made in the woodland at Goodwood, in Chichester, on the Channel coast and in other Sussex locations. However, like many works of art, it is not so simple: it is more than just an assemblage of audio and visual materials.

Two hollow stainless steel walls run parallel to one another for just over twelve metres, and along their length are positioned sound outlets, staggered so that they do not face one another. The surface of the steel is worked to a degree that it both reflects and absorbs the landscape, becoming part of it visually and aurally. As you move through this audio corridor you are met by different sounds - sounds which reflect the general environs where the sculpture is placed, used as a painter or sculptor uses physical matter. Furlong's stance is that of a sculptor who happens to use sound as the main ingredient of his art.

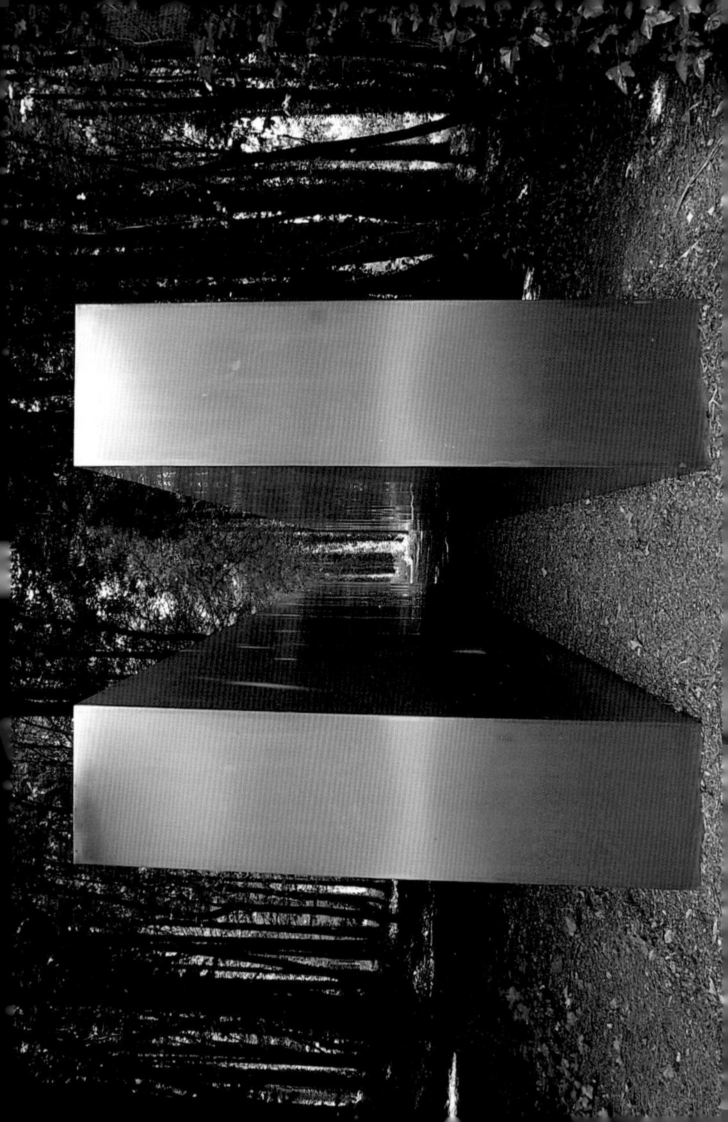

Jim Unsworth

Another Surprise for Fabricius Luscinus 1997-98
steel, painted, H 315
Enabled by Sculpture at Goodwood

Nellie the Elephant, who packed her trunk and set off for the circus, only to return to the jungle after her adventures, had an independence of mind which seems also to be reflected in these creatures that have recently made their way into Jim Unsworth's sculptural repertoire. Pyrrhus, the King of Epirus, took it upon himself to terrify a prisoner of equal rank by hiding an elephant in a tent and letting the animal burst out in front of the unfortunate warrior. Fabricius, however, stood his ground. This episode, which took place in the Punic Wars, is recorded in Plutarch and came to Jim Unsworth's notice after he made his first elephant sculpture where the beast is seen emerging from a striped circus tent. The application of story to existing sculpture denies an illustrative motive, indicating that Unsworth's approach to making the work was fresh and unfettered. He began this series as a natural development from earlier pieces in which the Indian Deity, Ganesh, was concealed in abstract form.

Like many contemporary sculptors since Henry Moore, Unsworth is not concerned with particular differences between abstract and figurative sculpture. Formal considerations of the one may equally be applied to the other. The way in which the box container almost gives birth to the emerging elephant, that bursting forth of energy, may be seen from one point of view as particularly elephant-like, but from another angle as a craggy, lumpen form escaping containment. The carefully constructed head and trunk, made from fresh steel sheet, cut and welded, characterises elephant skin to a fine degree and contrasts with the colourfully striped box which is reminiscent of the circus. The drum which precariously supports the whole structure is not a real elephant stand, but a form which Unsworth has reinvented from the kind of innocent interpretations that may be found in children's drawings, and the elephant emerges like the proverbial rabbit out of a hat.

Charles Hadcock
Caesura IV 1995
cast iron, H 500 cm, edition 1/3
Enabled by Sculpture at Goodwood

Caesura: a pause near the middle of a line, or a break between words within a metrical foot, specifically in Greek and Latin poetry. *Caesura* for Charles Hadcock is a series of sculptures in which he explores and celebrates fragmentation, mathematics, multiplicity and the impossible. In *Caesura IV* the two fragments of a single sphere are turned against each other, making it impossible for the globe to be completed. It seems that if the eye were to carry the ascending curves to their conclusion, they would first form an arch, and then complete their circle under the earth. Furthermore, the blocks which form *Caesura IV* are all identical, apart from those at the edges where there are no bolt holes. Their placement suggests that they would complete a globe, but the fact that they do not diminish in size towards the poles makes this impossible. These twists in function are enjoyed by the artist as he alters the mathematics of the form, releases the geometry and then destroys the apparent function.

The plates of cast iron, bolted together with industrial precision, are made to the rules of the Golden Section (the division of a line so that the whole is to the greater as that part is to the smaller part), and in this case are based on the proportions of the artist's body. The outer skin is turned inwards showing the 'industrial' construction of multiple parts, thus turning on its head the logic with which the composition was formed. The textured surface is a celebration of man-made replicas of natural forms, as Charles Hadcock prefers to delve into areas first explored by others, the challenge posed by nature seeming too great. His abiding interest in mathematics, architecture, archaeology, the recent industrial past and manufacturing processes testifies to this.

Steven Gregory
Fish on a Bicycle 1998
bronze, H 177 cm, edition 1/9
Enabled by Sculpture at Goodwood

Norman Tebbit's maxim that we were all to get on our bicycles in order to find work has been taken to extremes by this fish out of water. Artists are renowned for putting together unlikely elements, and they have the power to realise the impossible in terms of their chosen material, in this case bronze. *Fish on a Bicycle*, out of his element, is as much a buffoon as Toad of Toad Hall. He has the appearance of showing off, but also exhibits a self-conscious air, conspicuous in the curl of his lip and the direction of his eye.

Bronze is the material of monuments, of serious art. Not only has Steven Gregory chosen to subvert the sculptural elements of fish and of bike by putting them into an unlikely and faintly ridiculous relationship and situation, but he has also subverted the material in this context. Bronze, however, gives the sculpture status. Details in fish-scale and fin would not appear as crisp in fibreglass as they do in bronze, and the patina, green for the fish, is applied with a painterly sensitivity. The matt blackness of the bicycle serves, by contrast, to demonstrate the versatility of this wonderful material.

Artistic play, or licence, lies in Gregory's selection of a real bicycle to support its hand-crafted rider. The bicycle has given the sculpture human scale, therefore the fish has human scale and his anthropomorphic nature is accentuated by the introduction of this real element. Having given the fish such status, anything is possible. Movement is implied as fins touch the pedals. This sculpture might well be the start of a long and imagined narrative, different for every viewer. Perhaps this giant among fish found the bicycle thrown into his pond, and decided to have an adventure exchanging water for air and the open road instead of murky depths. It is possible, however, that the role of the sculpture is to make us stay a while, and smile at the possibilities and at the comedy therein.

Bill Woodrow

Endeavour: Cannon Dredged from the First Wreck of the Ship of Fools 1994
bronze, L 440 cm
Enabled by Sculpture at Goodwood

> The world of fools has such a store,
> That he who would not see an ass
> Must bide at home and bolt his door,
> And break his looking glass. Anon

This is the tenth sculpture in a series devoted to the theme of the 'Ship of Fools', a commentary on the foolishness of mankind wrapped in wry humour. Uncomfortably penetrating insights into human frailty and our seeming inability to learn from experience are all present in *Endeavour.* At first sight the bronze cannon looks real and convincing, a traditional weapon of war with its terrible ammunition placed in a pile close by and ready for use. On closer inspection, however, the image falls apart. The cannon balls are representations of our world. The gun-barrel is the trunk of a tree, sprouting a leafy growth; it is supported by a crouching 'stick' man, sexually well endowed. Potential movement is found to be impossible as the wheels could not possibly work. They are metaphors for aspects of human life. Books represent an accumulation of knowledge from which we seem not to learn and here become dubious supports. A reel of cord, staked to the ground so that forward motion would cause it to unwind, hints at futility. A drum, the skin of which is pierced so that it could not possibly be played, is supported by a spindle which is a burning candle and would soon cease to exist. The last, a tray of food to keep the prisoner alive, has a axle which is a flute for music to feed the mind. A prisoner? Well, yes, the undercarriage appears to be a prison door. Music sustains us, the prisoner plays a rousing tune on his accordion, the wolf/dog (the head of the man/man's friend?) bites its own leg.

William Pye

Miss Prism 1998

stainless steel, water, H 500 cm, edition 1/5

Enabled by Sculpture at Goodwood

Water moving in a thin veil with incredible speed over polished stainless steel comes between us and our reflection and the reflection of the landscape, serving only to increase the magical quality of *Miss Prism*. Contrary to the landscape, the pristine reflective nature of the metal absorbs the atmosphere, and when viewed in sunny conditions the sculpture appears to be lit from within by pools of reflected light.

William Pye has consummate mastery over water and metal, and combines them in ways observed in nature. He saw water running over the surface of a mountain road, forming the sort of lace-like patterns that skim over the metal surface of Miss *Prism*. The sculpture has three vertical surfaces, each reflecting the woodland and the visitors who decide to come close. The sculpture has a bold presence because of its material quality which, ironically, in some lights serves as a disguise.

Not only is a prism a vertical rectilinear form, it also becomes a transparent body in this sculpture. In certain lights it appears to be a clear wall of water forever falling and refracting light. The sound of falling water out of doors refreshes not only the eye, but the mind and the soul.

Tony Cragg
Pillars of Salt 1998
bronze, H 500 cm, edition 1/2
Enabled by Sculpture at Goodwood

During a recent residency at the Henry Moore Studios at Dean Clough in Halifax, Tony Cragg was given space and time in which to develop ideas for new sculptures, without pressure for immediate results or for an exhibition. This unconditional generosity of The Henry Moore Sculpture Trust resulted in some remarkable sculptures formed in clay and cast in plaster. Vessel forms, towering, one on top of the next, grew into columns as mysterious as any primitive totem. On drying, salts emerged from the pink plaster to form encrustations on the surface of the vessels, like so much hoar-frost.

Pillars of Salt, made especially for Sculpture at Goodwood, emerged from the ideas Cragg worked on at Dean Clough. As much as *Trilobites* 1989, which graced Goodwood during its first three years, *Pillars of Salt* speaks of evolution and of change - this time of change in mineral growth and change through time. These versions of laboratory vessels, placed in linear vertical formation, are disguised by their proximity; stacked and conjoined, they become something new.

The clustering of different forms, which by their association tell a new story, is familiar territory in Cragg's working practice. The move forward with *Pillars of Salt* is the formality with which the separate elements are brought together - no random virus this, but steady, geometric growth.

The bronze surface is raw, left just as it emerged on cooling from the sand mould. Surface veins where the heat cracked the damp sand can be seen clearly, as can burnt parts where the molten metal reacted with the sand. The bronze has been left to patinate itself through time, much as the plasters at Dean Clough were allowed to develop their salt patina when this series began.

Cathy de Monchaux

Confessional 1997-98

copper, steel, glass, limestone, suede, H 500 cm

Enabled by Sculpture at Goodwood

This structure began over two years ago in the mind's eye of Cathy de Monchaux. She desired to make a place which was a sculpture and which was complete only when people came into it and conversed within its walls. Her reflective method of working has resulted in a building that is simple, assured and which looks from the outside to be a place without pretension, but with strength of line and solidity of form. Early ideas for this piece expressed in copious drawings and texts showed a more complex structure, spikily decorative and with notions of romance, of truths to be told and those which dare not be voiced. Through the long period of reworking her thoughts about this sculpture-place, Cathy de Monchaux eventually found that some constituents she had rejected - decorative pillars - which here are realised as simple vertical and horizontal members to support the glass sheets, were actually present in the form of reflections made by the screen which divides the space in two. Like most of de Monchaux's work, *Confessional* is secretive, it hints at comfort - here is a place to rest, to recline and to converse. It is quiet inside, away from the hustle of the crowd, but you could easily damage your hand on the spikes which are part of repeated hand shapes forming the decorative screen. The screen itself is a metaphor for all that confuses communication. Is my truth your truth? Do you understand me? Do I know you? We appear to communicate, but do we really? This screen is also a fretwork of rusting steel, gaining a patina through age and use, qualities which de Monchaux desires and celebrates in her work. *Confessional* is a place to rest on a walk through Goodwood's twenty-acre grounds, to shelter and to talk.

Victoria Rance
Ark 1997
galvanised steel, H 500 cm
The Artist

Although this sculpture is in effect an apse, a protective space for a figure to stand inside, Victoria Rance took as her inspiration the form of a mediaeval chest used to hold vestments and other treasures in a Norfolk church. The chest was carved from oak and had a curved top. When Rance embarked on the sculpture, her intention was to make a containing space, and the chest form became instead an architectural one - a space for a saint, or for a human, a precious being. The curved top exhibits a sunburst, the equivalent of a halo in a religious painting or sculpture.

Galvanised steel rods welded close together form the curved wall which shields the figure. Similar rods are worked on in a more open way for the halo whilst completing the volumetric space. The technical requirements in this sculpture are basic, the materials are simple, but the finished work conveys ideas far beyond these simple means.

Victoria Rance also engages mathematics in her work. The circle features frequently. Materials with linear qualities - rods, wires, reeds and bristles - are frequently incorporated. She enjoys the result of gathering a bunch of reeds into a tight bundle, but allowing the ends to spring free, to arrange themselves. Similarly she anchors wires to a solid form, allowing them to indicate volume through the way they react to gravity. Whilst these particular techniques are not employed in *Ark*, Rance has taken the experience of working such materials into this sculpture. Henry Moore explored ways of a vulnerable form being protected by a stronger, outer one. His sculptures on the theme of Madonna and Child have the spiritual dimension which Victoria Rance seeks in her work, but with different means and within the context of a younger generation.

Bryan Kneale
Deemster Fish 1996
corten steel, L 366 cm
Enabled by Sculpture at Goodwood

Deemsters are the judges of the Isle of Man, who, when reciting how they will carry out the laws of the island, promise to do so 'as evenly as the spine of the herring lies between its flesh'. The herring, historically the staple food of the island's people, has become a symbol of good, and Bryan Kneale, himself a Manx man, has used the form of the herring in this sculpture. He was commissioned by the Deemsters to make a sculpture for their court building in Douglas, and he spent the last eighteen months or so investigating the nature of the fish, and relating it to one of three possible sites in and around the building a wall, a ceiling and an open outdoor area. He found over fifty possibilities in drawings and in metal models, and decided that a structure to hang on a particular wall in the courthouse was the best solution. The wealth of ideas related to the subject meant that Sculpture at Goodwood was able to help him realise a free-standing version.

Kneale developed the form as an 'inside/outside' structure in which both the exterior and inner workings of the fish were conveyed without being too literal. The many models and drawings he made varied in emphasis from mechanistic, possibly very abstract solutions to others which conveyed more movement. The Goodwood piece is the most abstract. An inclination towards investigating skeleton forms in animals, birds and reptiles is well established in Kneale's vocabulary, and these pieces are both complex and mature.

The model for *Deemster Fish* is exactly like the finished sculpture. Bryan Kneale has a strong sense of scale in his work, which allows his models to be enlarged precisely. The flexibility and resilience found in corten steel allows the form in this sculpture to remain precise - a softer, polished metal would not hold the shapes so exactly.

Zadok Ben-David
Conversation Piece 1996
bronze, L 366 cm, edition 1/6
Enabled by Sculpture at Goodwood

In the early 1990s, Zadok Ben-David, who had been making animal sculptures with human attributes, turned his thoughts towards the opposite notion: the idea of the beast within man. But there is, in addition, landscape within the form. The horizontal line drawn along the back to the head of this crouched figure forms a horizon on which cavorting figures describe his inner self. Zadok Ben-David has created something he calls an 'inner-scape'. It is not a self-portrait.

This figure was first made as an outline drawing in metal rods, then fleshed out with wire mesh and covered with a textured coating of resin. The inner figures are drawn and cut in aluminium with a jig saw - 'almost quicker than drawing for me now,' says Ben-David. In this case, the whole was then cast in bronze.

The silhouette form is typical of Zadok Ben-David's sculpture. It came from his use of shadows in earlier work, for example, *The Lizard Hunter Who Has Been Followed by His Own Shadow* and *The Marvellous Adventure of A Yellow Elephant,* both of 1985. The shadows were just one element in a work, but have since become the whole sculpture. In their likeness to shadows, these new sculptures are black and have only a hint of three-dimensional form.

Andrew Sabin
Land-Bin 1998
galvanised steel, H 700 cm
Enabled by Sculpture at Goodwood

Andrew Sabin devised a series of sculptures, open containers like this, which would be placed on beaches surrounding the Atlantic Ocean. Passers-by would be encouraged to toss flotsam and jetsam into these gigantic bins, thereby performing the dual role of beach comber and artist. Their random and unpredicted activity completes the work, and sculptures would differ according to the sort of rubbish swept up on to the beach.

In cities such a sculpture would be impossible because of the kind of rubbish which accumulates. Smelly cartons and discarded food containers would attract vermin, and instead of assuming a random beauty, the bins would acquire qualities of nuisance proportions.

Land-Bin is different. Liking very much the form of the *C-Bins*, Andrew Sabin's bins for the beach, Sculpture at Goodwood suggested placing such bins within a woodland setting to see what would happen with the massive amounts of garden refuse that might be placed in the containers. Two semicircular bins, each half completing a vast open circular form, now receive fallen branches, grass cuttings and weeds. The gardeners are completing the sculptures which are beginning to take on solid form with layers of twigs and grass, an aesthetic in accordance with the needs of woodland maintenance.

The galvanised steel construction of *Land-Bin* has overtones of agricultural utilities and as a sculpture it occupies a unique place within the context of basic, everyday tasks.

Stephen Cox
Granite Catamarans on a Granite Wave 1994
black and white granite, L 800 cm
Enabled by Sculpture at Goodwood

When Stephen Cox first arrived in India in 1985 and travelled to the coastal village of Mahabalipuram, which is devoted to the production of traditional Indian temple carving, he was much taken with the fishing boats that were drawn up on the beach, and which, daily, plied a hazardous course in the strong currents of the Indian Ocean. Cox spent several months working with carvers in Mahabalipuram, preparing his own sculpture for the Sixth Indian Triennale, an international exhibition held in New Delhi, at which he won a major prize.

Cox set up his own studio near the sea on the road between Mahabalipuram and Madras, and has supported a small team of assistants there ever since. Continuing to be interested in the forms of the fishing boats, he bought several of them which he kept at his studio with the thought that one day he might be able to use them. Ten years later the image of these vessels has appeared in this sculpture. The granite catamarans are an exact replica of the wooden craft, carved planks that are bound together with cord. The solution Cox found to indicate the wave was achieved through drawing with a computer, and resulted in a grid of vertical columns made to varying heights. Granite from the quarries at nearby Kanchipuram was selected in two different colours, black for the boats and white for the wave.

Placed at the edge of Hat Hill Copse, the sculpture refers not only to the plantation with its even rows of trees, but also to the distant Channel coastline, as from some angles the boats appear to sit upon the watery horizon. The sculpture marks a new phase in Cox's development, in which he appears to be evolving an interest in sculpture as installation.

William Tucker
Frenhofer 1997
bronze, H 210 cm, edition 1/6
Enabled by Sculpture at Goodwood

The title is taken from Balzac's 1831 story *The Unknown Masterpiece*, later illustrated by Picasso and celebrated by Dore Ashton in her book *A Fable of Modern Art*. In the novel, the painter Frenhofer has for years been engaged in secret on a work which is eventually revealed to be a confusion of colour and line with the model's foot the only recognisable element. The story is a prophetic description of the risks of public incomprehension and of doubt or self-deception on the part of the modern artist.

Tucker's *Frenhofer* is at first sight a formless lump, suggestive of cloud or rock formations, but which on closer inspection seems to resolve itself into a torso, either that of a pregnant woman or of a paunchy male like Rodin's *Balzac* studies. The possibility of many images, and the risk of none at all - of total chaos - is for Tucker a consequence of the art of modelling, with shape and surface generated by the contact of the hand with the soft material. Over the past fifteen years the process of modelling has become as much the subject of Tucker's sculpture as it is the means. Gradually he has sought a more explicit image of the body which is as much sensed internally as from the outside.

Several years ago Tucker was invited by the Henry Moore Institute to work at the studio in Dean Clough. Models and drawings were sent from Tucker's studio in the United States and a preliminary core was prepared. In the event Tucker modelled the sculpture in a brief but intense period in April 1996 in a studio at West Surrey College of Art and Design in Farnham, and Sculpture at Goodwood underwrote the casting in bronze. The location at Goodwood was chosen by the artist for its combination of an intimate space enclosed by trees and the possibility of longer views.

Bill Woodrow

Sitting on History I 1990-95
bronze, L 300 cm, edition 1/10
Sculpture at Goodwood with a grant from The Henry Moore Foundation

Sitting on History I was purchased in celebration of Sculpture at Goodwood winning the National Art Collections Fund Prize 1996. This work brings together in one piece the strands of our main endeavours, to provide both major sculpture and excellent seating for the interest and enjoyment of our visitors.

This sculpture was proposed in response to a commission first mooted in 1990, and Bill Woodrow's Tate Gallery exhibition in 1996 gave him the opportunity to realise one of three ideas for sculptures which could function as seats. Woodrow had made three maquettes based on a book form: this version, one with coins as the seat backs, and another featuring two crows on the spine of the book fighting over a gold coin. His idea was to have a sculpture that was only completed conceptually and formally when a person sat on it. *Sitting on History I*, with its ball and chain, refers not as one might expect directly to chained libraries, but to the book as the captor of information from which we cannot escape. All of history is filtered through millions of pages of writing, making the book the major vehicle for years of research and study. Woodrow proposes that although we absorb this knowledge, we appear to have great difficulty in changing our behaviour as a result.

The real books from which the original maquettes were made came from a box of books given to Bill Woodrow by a London bookseller, discarded as no longer saleable. To Woodrow's wry amusement, in this haul were three volumes on the history of the Labour Party, which he chose to use for the maquettes. Woodrow finds books one of the most powerful democratic tools in the world and still possibly the most advanced form of communication - perversely more so than computers which seem now to dominate our lives.

Peter Burke
Host 1996
reclaimed copper, corten steel, H 190 cm, edition 1/3
Enabled by Sculpture at Goodwood

This legion of forty cloned figures, identical within, dissimilar without, stand in a mute encounter with their viewers. Their unseeing eyes, incomplete limbs and torsos are formed much as a chiffon scarf might describe features when blown by the wind across a face, or as leather urged and creased into the profile of a Venetian carnival mask over a wooden last. In many ways the fabrication process used by Peter Burke to make *Host* is similar. Burke collected used copper water tanks, and having removed the lime scale, he selected portions to be pressed against two metal press tools, shaped to form the front and back halves of the male human figure. The resulting shells were riveted together to make the whole. The pressure required to make the form 'read' in the copper was so great that it could only be done with an industrial press, in this case with one used in the production of aircraft parts at Dowty Aerospace in Wolverhampton.

But what is this multitude? Why are they here? What are they doing? Turned together, looking at each other, forming intimate groups, they would be benign and social like people at a cocktail party. Facing towards us, emerging en masse from the trees, they are confrontational, threatening, potentially enveloping, even suffocating. A host of angels might be both fearful to behold yet 'good' in intent - possibly this thought can be applied to these humanoid forms. The scale and distribution of the figures matches that of the trees and they work with the horizontality of the landscape rather than against it. The manner in which the figures emerge from the woodland was also important to Burke, as some are barely visible whilst others stand in full view. The organic and the mechanical merge in *Host* through Peter Burke's introduction of chance into the process of industrial replication, an area which he is continuing to investigate.

David Nash
Two Charred Vessels 1997
charred chestnut, H 650 cm
Large Oak Throne 1997
charred oak, H 575 cm
Charred Sphere, Cube and Pyramid 1997
charred oak, L 300 cm
Enabled by Sculpture at Goodwood

Native Sussex woods, oak and chestnut, were chosen by Nash from the Goodwood Estate woodyard, and further pieces, in particular the tree that forms *Large Oak Throne,* were purchased from the local English Woodland yard at Cocking to make these sculptures.

The clearing at the south-east corner of Sculpture at Goodwood was chosen by Nash for these works, selected because it is partly enclosed but with a long view over the cornfields to the distant coastline, affording dramatic changes of light and mood according to the time of day, the season and the weather. The installation is of three individual sculptures, all typical of Nash's oeuvre. *Large Oak Throne,* the largest throne form that David Nash has made in English oak, is carved from a single, massive tree, the breadth of the wood allowing the forms to take a generous sweep where gesture was given free rein. Against the open field and the sky *Sphere, Cube and Pyramid* stand in dramatic silhouette. Their intense blackness disguises the three-dimensional quality of the sculpture in some lights and from certain angles. These are the geometric forms used in the landscape paintings of Cezanne.

On entering or leaving the clearing one passes through two sentinel Vessels, both carved from single trunks of chestnut. Viewed against the trees, the works are returned to the place where they may well have grown. All of these sculptures were burned where they now stand, the process at once dramatic and controlled. When charred, the woods become anonymous.

Eilís O'Connell
Space Emptied Out 1994
stainless steel, corten steel, bronze, H 600 cm
Enabled by Sculpture at Goodwood

Space Emptied Out is a conundrum, a brain-teaser, a riddle even. Here are three objects, containers, whose presence suggest that they could hold things, perhaps liquids, in the bronze and corten steel structures. The basket weave of the stainless steel cord figure could contain solid things. The fact is, they contain nothing, not even 'space', we are told. As we think further, however, the forms themselves displace space by their mere existence. They occupy a specific area and the spaces between them are particular and consequently important to the composition as a whole.

The large and varied grain silos of an agricultural landscape can also be seen at work in *Space Emptied Out*, found, as here, in intimate clusters.

Of all the sculpture in the copse this alone defies precise description or analysis. It is indeed a conundrum.

Allen Jones
Temple 1997
steel, painted, corten steel, mosaic, H 8 m
Enabled by Sculpture at Goodwood

In his response to the artifice of cultivated landscape, Allen Jones sought to make a sculpture which used that artifice to distort scale and distance and to manipulate our perception of space, much as eighteenth-century landscape architects did when introducing decorative buildings and follies into their schemes. From far away the door to the temple suggests that a person may enter the inner space in comfort. The fact is that it is just over one and a half metres high, and an average adult has to stoop to get inside. This visual trick makes the sculpture larger than it is. This square building with its ziggurat roof could have been an elaborate plinth for a figurative sculpture. The four-square outer form gives lie to the inner space which is circular and with a conical ceiling that opens to the sky. The figure stands above, on a corner of the roof, so that from inside the pavilion it may be viewed from below, something akin to the experience of seeing someone on a high diving board from the depths of a swimming pool.

The figure itself is much more chunky than Allen Jones's aesthetic normally allows. The curves had to be gentle in order to receive the tessera of the mosaic - a more curvaceous form would have meant using much smaller pieces. To describe form with colour Jones asked the mosaicist to lay out ranges of tessera from yellow to red and from green to blue. They discovered that within the cooler portion of the spectrum the range was much larger than in the hotter hues. Jones has also used colour to introduce the notion of movement in the figure, with the alternate arms of yellow and green in diagonally opposing positions, indicating more an action for semaphore than that of a Hindu deity. This work is full of echoes - of past artistic practice, of other cultures, of other art forms, of the woodland landscape - made unconsciously, but discovered enroute.

Hamish Black

YP1 1998

brass, H 154 cm, edition 1/5

Enabled by Sculpture at Goodwood

Objects of identical volume may differ greatly in shape or surface area. A book when opened looks different and reveals more surface than it does when closed. If the cover is soft, the appearance changes when the volume is rolled. Through this simple act, supplemented by cutting and shaping, Hamish Black transformed a single copy of a Yellow Pages directory into the maquette which was the basis for *YP1*. Black took the directory and eased it into a shape which in horizontal cross-section made a key-hole. The pages splayed like mushroom gills, close at the centre, further apart at the outer edges.

Black's choice of brass for the enlarged sculpture is a playful acknowledgement of the colour of the directory's pages. When newly made the polished metal reflected, one sheet facing the next as in a hall of mirrors, and produced an impression of light glowing from within. The opposite was true of the book maquette, where the inner, more densely packed paper caused the centre to appear dark. The enlargement to a size where most people have to stand on tip-toe to look into the central cavity, shaped as a key-hole, helps to clarify our perception of the outer shape. Slowly, by looking at *YP1* from all angles, the ambiguous form becomes clear. The way Black has defined shape, volume, colour, texture and tone in this sculpture demonstrates that the most simple activity - that of rolling paper and cutting it - can evolve into an object of beauty and some curiosity. Here is a sculpture that is constructed, but which results from carving. It is a form that speaks of volume, yet is fragile, one that indicates lightness, but is heavy. *YP1* communicates new messages from those in the source document, although both may be 'read'.

Paul Neagu
Unnamed (Eschaton) 1997
stainless steel, bronze, D 200 cm
Enabled by Sculpture at Goodwood

This sculpture is linked to a series of works started in 1983 which are illustrated in *Reorganisation of Nothing* published by Generative Art Trust, London, in 1996. Paul Neagu has a long-standing interest in eschatology, the theological doctrine concerned with death and final destiny, which for him generates speculative concepts of a cosmological future. In the material form of sculpture the highly reflective surfaces of stainless steel and polished bronze are appropriate vehicles to realise these concepts. Also the form they take - the circle and globe - at once infinite and finite, encourages the viewer to think beyond the physical reality of the work. Neagu writes that he is seeking, 'a transfigurative brightness, a tangible near-perfect paradise. The spheres are all marked with my name, the artist "me" is atomised, dispensable, potentially unstable as all universes are.'

The spheres are prefabricated boules, produced at a factory in Lyons, 'La Boule Integralé'. In this work they are a metaphor for atomic particles, and the fact that they are not made by the artist's hand is his way of depersonalising the subject. When asked about the colour in this sculpture, the warm bronze against the cooler steel, Neagu said that very rarely does he tamper with the natural colour of the materials he uses because he selects them with their natural qualities in mind.

'*Unnamed (Eschaton)* ... helps me to remember a minute golden bracelet made by an Etruscan craftsman (600 BC). I saw it at Villa Giulia in Rome. It contained a couple of hundred tiny lions, about 4 mm each. It also brings to mind a detail of a relief sculpture by Nicola Pisano (born c.1220) in the Duomo in Sienna which contains a small area of about forty portraits, part of the *Final Judgment*. Artists sometimes feel the need to express a preview of paradise... '

Michael Kenny
Belief and Desire 1997-98
Carrara marble, H 96 cm
The Artist

When titling his sculptures Michael Kenny intimates the need for quiet contemplation and an understanding of symbolism. This tactic provokes in us, the viewers, an interaction which steers our thinking and we come to the physicality of the sculpture with expectations which are likely to be different from those had we approached it knowing nothing. The forms are geometric, and Kenny's use of line is important in that it harmonises a sculpture made from separate elements.

In placing these solid forms on a base which is marked in a geometric configuration, similar to the lines he would draw on the studio or gallery floor when siting his work, he sets up points of connection with lines elsewhere in the sculpture, much as the maps which chart the heavens, where lines join stars in their different constellations. Michael Kenny is quoted in Peter Davies's book on his sculpture as saying, 'the large base plane isolates the figure in the sculpture, places it in a world apart - symbolic of psychological isolation.'

Carrara marble is one of the purest of white stones and its luminosity gives the sculpture a strong visual presence. Used by Michelangelo and sculptors of Classical Rome before him, it is imbued with historical connections. Kenny has taken the disparate forms of circle, arch and an L-shaped corner of a rectangle, and placed them in a comfortable relationship with the open 'L' towards the arched form raised slightly on its own marble disc. The surfaces are ground and polished to a smooth finish which contrasts with the roughly hewn edges giving visual bite to this carefully composed assembly. Vertical lines within both segments are coloured red and blue, painted by hand with a trembling motion, which harmonises with the portions of free carving.

Nigel Hall
Soglio (Goodwood) 1994
corten steel, L 1100 cm
Enabled by Sculpture at Goodwood

Soglio (Goodwood) 1994 was made some time after Nigel Hall had visited the Alps, and the site that he has chosen for the sculpture at Hat Hill reflects similar qualities in that landscape: a gap opening up, a far view, penetrating and broken forms. The rich patina of oxidised steel and the geometrically formal shapes contrast dramatically with the changing landscape. The great subtlety of line and angle to be found in this piece, Hall's largest sculpture to date, ensures that it rests well in its space. *Soglio* is the Italian word for throne.

'My work has always been about place, and for Goodwood the sculpture will echo the fracture in the broken wall,' said Hall, when planning this work. 'I like the idea of turning back and looking up the slope of the hill - a sense of engulfing and containment. I am fascinated by the way geometry can be discerned in landscape, and my preferred landscapes are mountains or the desert.

'The vertical form is the only vertical in the rolling landscape. It anchors the sculpture and relates to the viewer's vertical stance. It indicates the earth's centre. The break in the three wedge forms echoes the angled break in the long flint wall, while the truncated cone acts both as a lens and frame to focus and isolate various pockets of landscape.

'It's a meditative space, creating a ground in which the figure of the vertical can exist in stillness. The sculpture is still when the viewer is still but active when the viewer moves. For example, when moving across the face of the sculpture the vertical "knife blade" seems to open and close suddenly.'

Edward Allington

Fallen Pediment (Piano) 1994
copper, L 300 cm
Enabled by Sculpture at Goodwood

This is the only sculpture, so far, that Edward Allington has made to be shown in the open air. He was persuaded to do so by the qualities of light and colour that Hat Hill Copse had to offer, when towards the end of the day on his first visit to the copse the light falling through the trees shed a red glow over the green ground cover and the trees appeared to be as perfect as those in a Japanese garden. His choice of copper for the sculpture is reflected in his first impressions, although it is a metal that he loves and uses frequently.

Elements of architecture and the realm of classicism which are central to Allington's work are here in *Fallen Pediment*, the concept for which at first seemed to be relatively simple. He planned to make a form which appeared to be resting lightly on the ground, with a modest presence that you might miss should you not be looking carefully. When he began to draw the slightly roofed pediment shape, distorted by pulling it round in a horizontal plane, he thought that the resolution would be straightforward. 'I started to try to draw it and although I could make quite reasonable freehand sketches of the way I thought it might be, drawing in a technical manner always failed. I presumed my technical draughtsmanship was not up to it, so I did not worry about it.' However, when he began to work with sheet metalworkers they all began to realise how problematical the construction was going to be. He also made a cardboard structure which failed in the same way as the drawings, but slowly the work was resolved, revealing in the process the tricks that stonemasons employ when carving pediments for buildings.

Sculptors' Biographies

Edward Allington

Edward Allington was born in Troutbeck Bridge, Westmorland (now Cumbria) in 1951. He studied at Lancaster College of Art (1968-71), the Central School of Art and Design, London (1971-74) and the Royal College of Art, where he read cultural history (1983-84). He was prizewinner of the John Moore's Liverpool Exhibition (1989) and Gregory Fellow in Sculpture at Leeds University (1989).

Allington's first solo exhibition was at 1b Kensington Church Walk, London, in 1977. Since then his work has been shown frequently in both mixed and one-man exhibitions in many countries, including Japan, America and throughout Europe. He lives and works in London.

A long-standing interest in Greek and Roman cultures is evident in Edward Allington's sculpture and drawing. References to architectural detail, collectors' artifacts, placement and social context also play their part, and the viewer soon realises that there is a sense of deep enquiry as well as a little mischief at play. In his early work Allington explored a wide variety of materials, but recently he has used copper and bronze, sometimes with other elements, such as photographs of the work in a non-museum context.

Zadok Ben-David

Zadok Ben-David was born in Bayhan, Yemen, in 1949, and was brought up in Israel. He studied at Bezalel Academy of Art and Design, Jerusalem (1971-73), Reading University (1975) and St Martin's School of Art, London (1976). When he moved to London to study he not only had to come to terms with a new verbal language, but also a new visual language - British abstraction and conceptual art of the 1970s was very different from that in Jerusalem. At that time, leading British sculptors such as Anthony Caro, Phillip King and Tim Scott were teaching at St Martin's. After two intensive years of study, Ben-David found himself alone in a Greenwich studio and felt the need to come to terms with his own identity through his work - a search for meaning rather than working intuitively. He acknowledged everything that he found in his adopted culture, but selected carefully those aspects that would bring greater meaning to his work as an artist.

Colour and animal forms are characteristic of Zadok Ben-David's early work. The remembered warmth of the Yemeni desert comes through in warm yellows and reds, and the animals, recalled largely through childhood stories, play out their mythical tales. Textured surfaces absorb the light and help the colours to resonate, and the contrast of matt black shadows enable the forms to flatten. In recent work the role of the animal has altered. Instead of examining anthropomorphic animal activity, Ben-David has turned to looking at the animal in man. Man's beastly qualities are indicated by his stance and actions. Metaphysics has drawn Ben-David to an interest in the alchemist and man's scientific discoveries in the eighteenth and nineteenth centuries. Scientific book illustrations from this time also hold a great interest for him, and have found their way into his installation work. All of these focus on an underlying interest in man, his humanity and his progression in the world.

Hamish Black

Hamish Black was born in Braintree, Essex, in 1948. He studied at Eastbourne School of Art (1965-67), at North East London Polytechnic (1967-70) and at the Slade School of Art, University College, London (1970-72).

Black's origins as a sculptor lie in childhood experiences of his father's blacksmithing business, and in the influence of early works by Reg Butler and David Smith. Seven years of professional training were followed by a sustained period of teaching which enabled him to make sculpture - pieces which were largely site-determined, mostly large timber constructions in rural locations. Throughout his career Hamish Black has continued to teach part-time, which supports his professional studio practice. He is currently senior lecturer at the Kent Institute of Art and Design and sculptor supervisor for the MA course on site specific sculpture at Wimbledon School of Art.

A strong figurative content has persisted in Hamish Black's sculpture. Found objects and scrap metals contributed their own identity to early works in which Black sought to achieve vital and new relationships. His acceptance of a watering can or dustbin being integral to a sculpture allowed him to develop these relationships as metaphors for ideas. He found that the addition of objects of particular scale on a one-to-one basis could be altered when some components were scaled up or scaled down. This new element in his work caused a transition in perceived relationships - a spoon, for example, may be made unreasonably larger than its cup and saucer. Recently, the materials collected by Hamish Black as sources for his work are translated into new forms. Folded, rolled, layered and cut, they are endowed with a new reality which may finally be realised in other materials - bronze, brass or steel - or made to a larger scale. Hamish Black exhibits his work regularly, and is represented in public and private collections including South East Arts and Brighton Borough Council. He lives and works in East Sussex.

Peter Burke

Peter Burke was born in London in 1944. On leaving school he entered a student apprenticeship with Rolls Royce, Bristol (1960-65), then trained as a teacher at Bristol Polytechnic (1965-68) and studied for one year in the Fine Art Department there (1972-73). Whilst working as a teacher of art and design Burke maintained his practice as an artist, and for the last five years has given his time fully to his work as a sculptor.

The human form has long been a preoccupation in his work, and is expressed in many ways in his sculpture - fragmented, whole, in groups or singly. Burke's engineering background has given him an interest in industrial working methods and structural systems which he incorporates into his work. He enjoys replication and mass production and employs these processes. In his work the random meets the controlled and precision encounters chance.

Drawing is important to Burke as a way of working up ideas for sculpture, envisaging relationships between his figures rather than their full form which takes its chance in the making.

Peter Burke has exhibited his work since 1973 in mixed shows, his first being the Cheltenham Festival's exhibition of sculpture in the open air. His first solo exhibition was at South Hill Park, Bracknell (1978), since when he has shown regularly at international art fairs and in British and overseas galleries. Peter Burke is represented by the New Art Centre Sculpture Garden and Gallery where he has shown his sculptures since the early 1990s.

His work is in private collections in Britain, Europe and the United Sates, and has also been acquired by the Contemporary Art Society, London (Henry Moore Foundation purchase). Peter Burke lives and works in Bradford on Avon, Wiltshire.

Sir Anthony Caro

Sir Anthony Caro was born in New Malden, Surrey, in 1924. He studied engineering at Christ's College, Cambridge (1942-44). After National Service with the Fleet Air Arm of the Royal Navy (1944-46), he attended Regent Street Polytechnic Institute, London (1946) and the Royal Academy Schools, London (1947-52).

Caro worked as a part-time assistant to Henry Moore (1951-53), and taught part-time at St Martin's School of Art, London (1952-1980). There he virtually formed what was to become an influential Department of Sculpture where young artists, following his lead, were working in new materials such as plastic and fibreglass as much as, or more than steel. Caro's early sculpture was figurative and expressionistic, worked in clay and cast metals. In 1959 he broke away from figuration and made works from scrap steel girders and sheet metal, welded and bolted together. Many were coated with industrial and household paints. His first table sculptures were made in 1966. Smaller than previous work, these reclaimed the pedestal in a different form and were made well into the 1980s. Meanwhile he was developing his work in steel on a massive scale, some of which is essentially architectural. In 1993 Caro returned to working with clay in combination with metal and wood (having worked twice before with clay and ceramics) in a series of sculptures describing the Trojan Wars, his first semi-figurative work since the 1950s.

Anthony Caro has had numerous exhibitions throughout the world, from the first *Biennale des Jeunes Artistes* in Paris in 1959 where he won the sculpture prize, to his magnificent retrospective exhibition at the Trajan Markets in Rome in 1993. His work is well known and respected from the United States to Japan, and in 1995 a large retrospective exhibition was shown at the new Metropolitan Museum of Art in Tokyo, the museum's first exhibition offered to a foreign artist. He was awarded a knighthood in the Queen's Birthday Honours 1987.

Lynn Chadwick

Lynn Chadwick was born in London in 1914. He attended the Merchant Taylor's School, and after taking his School Certificate stayed on to study drawing, watercolour and oil painting. He was then sent to Vouvray to study French. From 1933 to 1939 he trained and worked as an architectural draughtsman in London.

In 1940-41 he worked as a farm labourer and then volunteered for the Fleet Air Arm, becoming a pilot and gaining a commission. After the war he returned to his work with the architect Rodney Thomas, specialising in exhibition design. His early sculptural works took the form of mobiles, which he began to make in 1947, having moved from London to Gloucestershire. A mobile constructed from aluminium and balsa wood was shown at the Aluminium Development Stand at the Builders' Trades Exhibition that year. At this time, and until 1954, he produced textile, furniture and architectural designs.

Chadwick's first one-man exhibition was held at the Gimpel Fils Gallery, London, in 1950, the first of many exhibitions world-wide. These have included the XXVIII Venice Biennale of 1956 where he won the International Sculpture Prize, one of many awards and accolades, including the CBE in 1964. Early in his career he worked occasionally to commission, but less as he became established.

His approach to making sculpture is based in construction rather than modelling. Chadwick first makes a linear armature or skeleton before building on a solid skin. The work might be unique or made to a predetermined edition by casting or fabrication. Chadwick has created a permanent exhibition of his work at his Gloucestershire home, Lypiatt Park, and also a foundry, Pangolin, which casts not only his sculpture but also work for many other artists.

Stephen Cox

Stephen Cox was born in Bristol in 1946. He studied at the Central School of Art and Design, London (1966-68).

Cox's work is based in other cultures. Rooted in classicism, his early sculptures related to architecture and archaic fragments, and were realised in stone from Italian quarries. The Mediterranean as the cradle of civilisation of the Western world provided the context and the substance for his work.

In 1986 Cox represented Britain at the Sixth Indian Triennale in New Delhi. He went to Mahabalipuram, a centre for traditional Hindu carving, to make sculpture for the exhibition, and since that time has maintained a studio there. The carvings he made in granite from the ancient quarries of nearby Kanchipuram were to have a great bearing on his work over the next decade. Some were more overtly 'Indian' than others, and might be viewed as being linked to the humanism of both the Eastern and Western worlds.

Another opportunity for Cox to work in a new context, this time in Egypt, presented itself in 1988. He was commissioned to carve sculpture for the new Cairo Opera House, and was allowed to quarry Imperial porphyry at Mons Porphyrytes in the Eastern Desert, which had not been used since the Renaissance. This in turn led to new developments in his imagery, such as references to the human torso. In varying his treatment of the rich red and green stones, Cox developed his sculpture towards a more abstract state. In 1993 he completed a commission for the parish church of St Paul, Harringay, using Italian and Egyptian stones.

Cox continues to work in Egypt and has been given permission to quarry stone from another ancient site, the Kephren Quarries in the Western Desert of southern Egypt.

Tony Cragg

Tony Cragg was born in Liverpool in 1939. He worked as a laboratory technician at the Natural Rubber Producers Research Association (1966-68) before attending Gloucestershire College of Art and Design, Cheltenham, and the Royal College of Art, London (1973-77). Tony Cragg has lived and worked in Wuppertal, Germany, since 1977.

An artist of great international acclaim and immense energy, Cragg has developed more possibilities in the making of sculpture than any other sculptor since Moore discovered the 'hole' as positive space. He has employed more materials than most, and tested them to their limits through a wide variety of means, so that he seems to be one hundred sculptors at any one time. However, the continuum in his work is strong and uncompromising. His concerns are for humanity, its direction, the life of our planet and its projected evolution. Cragg's contribution to the debate on contemporary sculpture practice is considerable, and has yet to be measured.

Early works of the 1970s were mostly made with found objects through which Cragg questioned and tested possibilities. Later pieces, sometimes derived from found materials, demonstrated a shift of interest to surface quality and how that could be manipulated, and a play with unlikely juxtapositions of materials. Results vary from the exquisite to the grotesque, from the refined to the crude, in bronze, steel, plastic, rubber, glass, wood, plaster and more.

Maggie Cullen

Maggie Cullen was born in Hastings in 1967. She studied three-dimensional design at Middlesex Polytechnic (1988-91) and is currently working for an MA in Visual Theory at the University of East London. Maggie Cullen's early work was centred in ceramics, and as she began to make sculpture in other materials she found a need to discover a more philosophical base for her work. The course in Visual Theory has provided access to both philosophy and psychology which she is beginning to find helpful in moving her work forward. She is particularly interested in Walter Pater's *Epiphanies*, and in the realisation that it is possible to experience intense moments of revelation or profound perception which seem more real than everyday experiences.

Maggie Cullen lives and works in Hastings, East Sussex. Living near the sea since childhood has had a significant effect on her work and is essential to her well-being - to her spirit. Experiencing the qualities of light and space found on the south coast of England is necessary to her vision, and is particularly important in her recent work in plastics. She also acknowledeges the influence of artists such as Anish Kapoor, James Turrell and Richard Wilson, both for their intellectual engagement in their work and for the calm qualities conveyed by their sculptures and installations.

Exhibiting her work regularly since 1991, Maggie Cullen has already, in her early career, had four solo exhibitions. She hopes in the winter of 1998-99 to show her work in Mumbai, India, where she plans a glass beach installation. This project is part of an artists' exchange and has been organised by the participating artists.

John Davies

John Davies was born in Cheshire in 1946. He studied painting at Hull and Manchester Colleges of Art (1963-67), after which he spent two years at the Slade School of Fine Art, London. He was awarded a sculpture fellowship at Gloucester College of Art in 1989 and in the following year he won the Sainsbury award. The most important solo exhibition for John Davies in his early career was held at the Whitechapel Art Gallery, London in 1972, followed by another at the same venue three years later. His most recent exhibition was at the Whitworth Art Gallery, University of Manchester, in 1995-96. His sculpture and drawings have been included in many group exhibitions in Britain, Europe, America, India, Australia and Japan with pieces being acquired in most of those countries for both public and private collections.

John Davies's sculpture and drawings are centred on the human figure. He has written, 'People are our whole world, sun, moon and stars.' Early figures were often arranged in carefully positioned relationships, playing out a silent drama through look and gesture. Gesture remains important in his single figures, where an extended hand or slight inclination of a head might indicate another presence. The presence of others may also be suggested by a small hand against a large face or several hands joined together. Heads, from small pieces that can be held between two fingers to giant heads like huge rocks, eroded by the wind and sea, demonstrate his skill with scale and drawing. Finely delineated features and well-worked textures indicate character and feeling(s) and many other aspects of the human condition.

The artist's own words best sum up his continued fascination with and explorations of the human form: 'My work has carried me closer to people - in a kind of circle. My sculpture seems to have that function for me. If it does the same for other people that would mean a great deal to me.' John Davies lives and works in Kent, having recently returned from living in northern Greece.

Iain Edwards

Iain Edwards was born in Heswall, Merseyside, in 1962. He studied at Wrexham College of Art, North Wales (1980-81), where he passed the foundation course with distinction and at West Surrey College of Art, Farnham (1981-84,) leaving with a BA Hons First Class degree.

His work is influenced by the townscape of London docklands, which being close to his studio he encounters daily. He addresses the importance of craftsmanship, and structures which are well built and designed. Since none of his works in which he propose the possibilities of movement or containment can fulfill that function, their fantastical elements are revealed. His fascination and obsession with the construction of the wheel is a major feature of his work, made all the more interesting when one learns that his great grandfather having emigrated from Germany in the nineteenth century, established a coach building company in Liverpool - a fact of which Edwards was ignorant until relatively recently.

Iain Edwards has exhibited his work in Germany and France as well as in London and Edinburgh, mostly in group shows, and with a solo exhibition at the Concourse Gallery in Archway, London, in 1989.

Edwards lives and works in London, sharing a studio in Bow with the sculptors Jim Unsworth and Philip Medley.

Nigel Ellis

Nigel Ellis was born in Old Stevenage in 1960, and studied at St Alban's College of Art (1978-79), Canterbury College of Art (1979-82) and Chelsea School of Art (1983-1984). He now lives and works in Shoreditch, in East London.

A series of events led to a decisive moment in Nigel Ellis's future career as a sculptor. In 1976 he saw the complete sculptures of Degas at the Lefevre Gallery, and he embarked on a course in 3D design. The idea of looking at an everyday object, in his case a water tap, as if it were transparent, drawing as though he could see the object from sides that were hidden, helped him to see things in a new way. The inner qualities of the Degas sculptures made him aware that material things carried elements which are invisible.

The body of work which followed was an attempt to externalise actual sensation as if the signals of the nervous system in certain significant poses were on view. This was the beginning of a quest which still continues. Ellis sees his work as a search for 'sustained awareness'. He wants to see 'sculpture that is an authentic and rigorous embodiment of experience without in any way depicting it'. He is also fascinated by the formal, imaginative and optical explorations of modernism, particularly in Britain, in the early sixties. His works have become increasingly architectural over recent years, and colour, geometry and repeated forms all have their place in his work.

Nigel Ellis was involved in the development of the Florence Trust which provides studio space for artists in London. He exhibits his work regularly and has recently made a series of computer enhanced photographs with the National Trust.

Ian Hamilton Finlay

Ian Hamilton Finlay was born in Nassau, Bahamas, in 1925. As a child he was brought to Scotland, where he attended boarding school. His education ended at the age of thirteen, when at the outbreak of war he was evacuated to the Orkney Islands.

A short spell at art school in Glasgow was followed by a period in London before Finlay joined the army in 1942. At the end of the war, he worked as a shepherd, studied philosophy, and began to write short stories and plays, some of which were broadcast by the BBC.

Much of Finlay's work has been made in collaboration with other artists and with artisans, and draws on his experience of rural life and the sea. His studies of classicism and ancient philosophers have enriched his work immeasurably.

At Stonypath, near Edinburgh, his home since 1966, Finlay has developed the garden to feature his concrete poetry and sculpture. Although he has gained a considerable international reputation through numerous exhibitions abroad, Ian Hamilton Finlay never travels away from his home.

William Furlong

William Furlong was born in Woking, Surrey, in 1944. He studied at Guildford School of Art and Crafts (1960-65) and then at the Royal Academy Schools in London, (1965-68). Like most artists of his generation, on leaving college Furlong worked part-time in art schools in order to support his studio practice. He taught at Epsom School of Art, at Ealing School of Art and Photography, and then at Wimbledon School of Art where he is now a member of the professorial research staff, working with postgraduate and research students in fine art.

On establishing his studio as a young graduate, Furlong continued to paint and to make sculpture, having started to make his first three-dimensional and mixed media work at the Royal Academy. Important exhibitions for him during this period were the *New Contemporaries* at the Tate Gallery 1997 and in the *Northern Ireland Open* and John Moore's *Liverpool Exhibition* in 1969.

In 1973 William Furlong established Audio Arts, a two-stranded project in which he recorded, edited and published (under the label Audio Arts) conversations of artists, and produced sound works. It was his intention from the outset that Audio Arts was a creative project, and the two activities continue to overlap, each enriching the other. This was Furlong's first substantial involvement with the voice. His sound works were exhibited in a series of exhibitions, including *Art for Society 1978* at the Whitechapel Art Gallery and in *The Sculpture Show* at the Hayward Gallery in 1982. Shows in 1998 include a solo exhibition in the Bregenz Kunstverein; *Sound Garden*, Serpentine Gallery, and *An Imagery of Absence* at the Imperial War Museum.

Furlong finds that his way of working - using sounds and the voice as materials - is a sculptural and creative process. It arose from his intimate association with the voice when editing interviews which are for him actual constructions.

Andy Goldsworthy

Andy Goldsworthy was born in Cheshire in 1956 and was brought up in Yorkshire. He studied at Bradford College of Art (1974-75) and Preston Polytechnic (1975-78).

After leaving college Goldsworthy lived in Yorkshire, Lancashire and Cumbria. He moved over the border to Langholm, Dumfriesshire, in 1985 and to Penpont one year later. This gradual drift northwards was due to a way of life over which he did not have complete control. However, contributing factors were opportunities and desires to work in these areas and reasons of economy.

Throughout his career most of Goldsworthy's work has been made in the open air, in places as diverse as the Yorkshire Dales, the Lake District, Grize Fiord in the Northern Territories of Canada, the North Pole, Japan, the Australian outback, St Louis, Missouri, and Dumfriesshire. The materials he uses are those to hand in the remote locations he visits: twigs, leaves, stones, snow and ice, reeds and thorns. Most works are ephemeral but demonstrate, in their short life, Goldsworthy's extraordinary sense of play and of place. The works are recorded as photographs. Book publication is an important aspect of Andy Goldsworthy's work: showing all aspects of the production of a given work, each publication is a work of art in its own right.

Some recent sculpture has a more permanent nature, being made in stone and placed in locations far from its point of origin, as for example *Herd of Arches* 1994. The series of chalk *Arches* made at Sculpture at Goodwood in 1995 are semi-permanent, given the fragility of the material, and are now sited indoors at Goldsworthy's studio in Dumfriesshire, to extend their life.

Steven Gregory

Steven Gregory was born in Johannesburg, South Africa, in 1952. He studied at St Martin's College of Art, London (1970-72), returning there to complete his BA (Hons) (1977-79). During the intervening years he was an apprentice stonemason to the company Ratty and Kett, working at Westminster Abbey and Hampton Court. He obtained City and Guilds Craft and Advanced Craft Certificates in stone masonry (1975 and 1976). In 1977 he won the Worshipful Company of Masons Prize.

Gregory chose this course of action because of his desire to learn how to use tools. In the early 1970s art schools in Britain devoted much time to the exploration of concepts in preference to developing craftsmanship, which Gregory found frustrating. Leicester Museum and Art Gallery purchased a sculpture from his BA exhibition at St Martin's, and at that time he was commissioned to make a work for Rio Tinto Zinc using machine tools produced by the company.

Stone carving features largely in Steven Gregory's sculpture, although he has also developed ideas in bronze and other media. His intention is to make work that cannot be disregarded, which sometimes results in harrowing images of the human condition. There is also a lighter side to his work where his humour emerges, although the viewer should still search in the shadows for there might still lurk the black dimension.

Stephen Gregory works to commission, and has recently been invited to undertake a large private project..

Charles Hadcock

Charles Hadcock was born in Derby in 1965. He studied at Gloucestershire College of Arts and Technology (1984-87) and at the Royal College of Art, London (1987-89). His degree show at the Royal College generated a good deal of interest in his work, and many encouraging comments in the press. The ideas he was then trying out in his sculpture - using multiple images and explorations of the ready-made - remain important in his work today. A background in engineering (his father was an engineer), an abiding interest in Victorian engineering and in mathematics have enriched those original preoccupations, and are all present in his current work. His is not entirely a cool and calculated art, but one that also has analogies with poetry and music.

Transformation also plays its part. Polystyrene packaging might be cast in bronze and repeated as a multiple (it is a multiple in the first place), artificial paving stones - mass produced - are found giving texture and repetitive form in some sculptures. The nuts and bolts of nineteenth-century engineered bridges are celebrated in his work, giving the underside of the sculpture equal importance with the rest. Geometry also plays a part, in particular the Golden Section, based on the coordinates of Hadcock's own body, as do the rhythm, pause, crescendos and calm of music. All of this culminates in bronze or cast iron. Hadcock uses factory casting for his sculpture in preference to fine art foundries, as he likes the basic qualities of the factory processes to come through in the sculpture, and in particular revels in the qualities of cast iron.

Charles Hadcock has exhibited regularly in group shows since 1987, and has had one-man exhibitions at 249 Long Lane, London (1991), the Crypt Galley, London (1992) and Reeds Wharf Gallery, London (1996). His work can be seen at BAA Gatwick Stirling Hotel, Melbourne Science Park, Cambridgeshire, ICI, and Allied Domecq.

Nigel Hall

Nigel Hall was born in Bristol in 1943. He studied at the West of England College of Art, Bristol (1960-64) and the Royal College of Art, London (1964-67). On graduating from the Royal College, Hall won a Harkness Fellowship, and until 1969 he lived and worked in Los Angeles, travelling in the USA, Canada and Mexico. His work is represented in numerous public, corporate and private collections in Britain and abroad. Hall's first one-man exhibition was held at the Galerie Givaudan, Paris, in 1967. It is interesting to note that fifty out of his seventy-two solo exhibitions held between 1967 and 1996 have been in galleries abroad in cities spread throughout the globe: New York, Los Angeles, Perth, Melbourne, Sydney, Tokyo, Zurich, Dusseldorf, Cologne and Rome, to mention only a few. This international exposure has led to his work being represented in around 100 public and corporate collections and numerous private collections abroad and in Britain.

In 1970 Nigel Hall produced his first tubular aluminium sculptures in which he explored ways of encapsulating space in a linear manner, thus manipulating our perceptions of it. A sense of place and placement have always been integral to his work, and shadows play a role equal to that of line, mass or void, as do changes of aspect from altered viewpoints. An almost minimal refinement and economy of means in Hall's work has recently given way to robust forms which still remain very carefully considered in their configuration. These refer obliquely to mountain landscape which alters dramatically when the viewer moves within it. Site specific projects have also featured regularly during Nigel Hall's career. These include a wall sculpture for the entrance to the Australian National Gallery, Canberra, 1992; a two-part wall relief in painted and gilded wood for the entrance of Providence Towers, Dallas, 1989; and a free-standing steel sculpture for the entrance to Thameslink Road Tunnel, London Docklands, 1993, his largest structure to date.

Nicola Hicks

Nicola Hicks was born in London in 1960 into a family of well-established artists. She studied at Chelsea School of Art (1978-82) and at the Royal College of Art (1982-85).

She took part in Christie's Inaugural Graduate Exhibition in 1982, but was able to project her precocious talent with astounding effect when Elisabeth Frink chose her, aged twenty-four, for the annual *Artist for the Day* exhibition at the Angela Flowers Gallery in 1984.

At a time when London was enjoying fame as the capital of punk culture and the art world was focused on abstract and conceptual art, with sculptures often conceived as 'installations', Hicks's interest in animal forms made her feel out of step with her contemporaries. However, the image of a life-sized dying bull made of straw and hessian was the beginning of a long-standing relationship with the Angela Flowers Gallery, where she held her first solo exhibition in 1985. Since then she has exhibited in Paris, India, Denmark, Sweden and Norway, and her works have been included in public collections in Japan.

Her early animal sculptures were often as imaginary as they were real, portrayed as sentient beings. With the birth of her son, William, Hicks turned also to human form. The extent to which life and art are inextricably linked for her was given new meaning when she insisted that he was born in her studio. Within days she began to model the form of her baby, and some of her most poignant works are a reflection of the emotional experience of becoming a mother for the first time.

Hicks's mature works examine the relationship of human beings and animals, who have, she maintains, precious qualities in common, 'the qualities we are deeply in touch with subconsciously and may be totally out of touch within our conscious state.'

Allen Jones

Allen Jones was born in Southampton in 1937. He studied at Hornsey College of Art, London (1955-59) and the Royal College of Art (1959-60) and returned to Hornsey to take a teacher training course (1960-61).

The early 1960s at the Royal College of Art witnessed the birth of British Pop Art (Pop Art first emerged in America in 1960). Allen Jones was one of a group of students which included Derek Boshier, David Hockney, RB Kitaj and Peter Phillips, who radically changed the face of British art with their precocious, unconventional and irreverent work which was based in popular culture - embracing new subject matter and new materials. Jones's preference was for glamour and style, and his aesthetic centred on beautiful women visualised erotically and stereotypically as in glossy magazines, advertisements and cartoon strips. Underpinned with a great mastery of colour and a consummate painting technique, Jones's work fluctuates between painting and sculpture. On a flat canvas painted forms appear sculptural and his three-dimensional works are painterly. He uses colour to describe form, at times with graphic precision, or conversely with an energy and freedom of gesture which is close to direct expression. Similar developments are evident in his printmaking.

Having sustained a long and successful career as an artist, developing his work at a consciously measured pace, Jones has remained central to British art. His work may be seen in many public places including the most fashionable restaurants. He has carried out commissions for the City of London (1987), the British Airport Authority, Heathrow Airport (1991), Chelsea and Westminster Hospital (1992-93) and Sir Terence Conran's Mezzo Restaurant (1996), among others.

Michael Kenny

Michael Kenny was born in Liverpool in 1941. He studied at Liverpool College of Art (1959-61) and the Slade School of Fine Art, London (1961-64). Throughout the 1970s he was a visiting lecturer at the Slade School and from 1983 to 1988 was Head of the Fine Art Department at Goldsmith's College, London. Since he graduated from the Slade, Kenny has had many solo and group exhibitions in Britain and abroad, including Europe, USA, South America, Japan, Hong Kong and Australia. Consequently, many public and corporate collections throughout the world hold examples of his work.

The creative acts of drawing and making sculpture seem, in Michael Kenny's work, to be indivisible. The physical qualities of line are to be celebrated, whether drawn on smooth or textured paper or across a piece of stone, whether made in graphite or coloured pigment. 'Drawing', for Kenny, 'is a means of understanding, of searching for order out of chaos through images.' Geometry, symmetry and asymmetry are concerns, both in drawing and in sculpture. Stones with differing qualities are sometimes brought together in one piece, the grainy dark greens and browns of Hornton stone contrasting with the cool, smooth texture of Portland stone or the warmer hue of Bath limestone. Recently Kenny has introduced blue-grey Killkenny marble and white Carrara marbles into his compositions, adding to the range of colour and surface quality in his sculpture. Strong diagonals and verticals in both solid form and in line, pull our attention towards the notions of gravity which are also vital in his work.

Michael Kenny was elected Associate of the Royal Academy in 1976 and Royal Academician in 1986. He lives and works in London.

Bryan Kneale

Bryan Kneale was born in Douglas on the Isle of Man in 1930. His early ambition was to be a painter, and he studied at Douglas School of Art (1947) and at the Royal Academy Schools (1948-52). In 1948 he won the Rome Prize, and spent most of his time travelling in Italy where he was greatly influenced by the work of the Futurists and metaphysical painters. On his return to London in 1951 he started painting with palette knives with a desire to construct in paint, the foundation of his gradual move towards working entirely in three dimensions. In 1960, having learnt welding techniques, Kneale abandoned painting and had his first exhibition of sculpture later that year.

Bryan Kneale has mostly constructed, forged and cast his sculpture himself. He has taught sculpture at the Royal Academy Schools, Hornsey College of Art and the Royal College of Art, where he was Senior Fellow in 1995, the year of his retirement.

His work is largely centred on organic form. Skeletons and joints of animals are explored through drawing and construction in metal. Kneale prefers to work directly in metal rather than modelling in an intermediary material before casting in bronze.

Exhibitions include regular one-man shows since 1953 and group exhibitions since 1961. Kneale has shown mostly in Britain, with occasional exhibitions abroad, although his work is represented in collections from Australia and New Zealand to Brazil and New York. In Britain his drawings can be found in the Natural History Museum and the British Museum, and his sculpture at the Tate Gallery and in many municipal and private collections.

Bryan Kneale was elected ARA in 1970 and Royal Academician in 1974. He lives and works in London.

David Mach

David Mach was born in Methil, Fife, in 1956. He studied at Duncan Jordanstone College of Art (1974-79) and at the Royal College of Art, London (1979-82). A random look at his biography shows a life full of activity. For example, in 1989 there are listed twelve exhibitions or installations in ten different cities, ranging from San Francisco to Madrid and Milton Keynes to Melbourne. This is typical of his hectic work pattern which built up to this pitch within four years of his leaving the Royal College, and continues unabated.

Multiple mass-produced objects, most notably magazines, newspapers and car tyres, have been used consistently by Mach throughout his career. He brings diverse items together in large-scale installations with humour and social comment. His work is representational and controversial. A work of the early 1980s, *Polaris* 1983, shown at the Hayward Gallery in London, took the form of a submarine, but made of used car tyres. This monumental tribute to nuclear power was set alight by highly critical viewers who obviously failed to see its irony.

David Mach's sculpture is on the verge of being completely overwhelming in its scale and audacity. Making classical pillars from thousands of newspapers and magazines at the Tramway Gallery in Glasgow in 1990 was a marathon of physical effort in which he was helped, as in much of his work, by his wife Lesley. Papers were fanned and stacked around existing supporting pillars in the tram sheds, transforming them to the scale and form of columns that would support the Acropolis. He also uses magazines to form swirling waves which carry other objects in their turbulence. The density of these installations is echoed in his smaller sculptures where multiple objects are used to make the whole. Typical are the 'match head' series: portraits, similar to Chinese and Venetian theatre masks, made from unstruck matches glued together so that only the coloured heads show on the surface. Sometimes these are fired to form faces of a sombre hue.

Dhruva Mistry

Dhruva Mistry was born in Kanjari, Gujarat, India, in 1957. He studied sculpture at the Faculty of Fine Arts, MS University of Baroda (1974-79), graduating with distinction and a gold medal. He went on to gain an MA at Baroda (1979-81) and then came to Britain on a British Council Scholarship to take an MA in Sculpture at the Royal College of Art (1981-83).

From 1983 to 1996 Dhruva Mistry pursued his career as a sculptor in Britain. He has residencies at Kettle's Yard Gallery, Cambridge, with fellowships at Churchill College (1984-85) and at the Victoria and Albert Museum, London (1988). He received many awards in this thirteen-year period, including the Third Rodin Grand Prize Exhibition, Japan (1990); the Jack Goldhill award (1991); the Humanities Prize medal award in the Asian Artist Today - *Fukuoka Annual VII,* Fukuoka, Japan (1994); the Design President's award for the Victoria Square Sculptures, the Landscape Institute and Marsh Fountain of the Year award for Victoria Square, Birmingham (1995). Dhruva Mistry was elected Royal Academician in 1991 and was made fellow of the Royal Society of British Sculptors in 1993. In 1997 Dhruva Mistry returned to India to live and work in Baroda.

The rich imagery and narrative content of Indian art, the highly developed skills of a dedicated sculptor, working in a culture not his own, and an independence of mind which channels effort absolutely, have all contributed to Dhruva Mistry's success as a sculptor. His work ranges from huge public commissions to maquettes and wall reliefs, related in part to Hinduism and Buddhism, but also encompassing influences from the West - Egyptian and Cycladic art and European traditions of figurative sculpture. Not all his sculpture is narrative. In some work he explores the processes of making art and the inevitable intellectual debate that ensues between artist and viewer, whether implied or expressed.

Cathy de Monchaux

Cathy de Monchaux was born in London in 1960. She studied at Camberwell School of Art, London (1980-83), and at Goldsmiths' College, London (1985-87).

In her sculpture, Cathy de Monchaux combines opposites. Hard and rough contrast with smooth and soft, as she places brass and steel against leather and velvet. The forms also work in opposition, with spikes or jagged edges contrasting with sumptuous curves and padded surfaces. Her imagery is sexual, hinting at the bordello and all that it voluptuously implies. The harshness and softness of nature which simultaneously attract and repel - the Venus fly-trap in action - are both present in the unspoken danger.

As the substance of de Monchaux's work becomes more complex, more vivid, the linear motifs recall Islamic architecture. Trapped between two thick sheets of glass, drawings on a translucent ground are at the same time studies and objects. The decorative clamps and bolts which hold the glass together are the brutality; the fluid line is the grace. In recent installations she has added ephemeral elements such as patterns of powder or dust which appear as shadowy traces of her sculptural forms. These traces add a sense of history and of decay.

Cathy de Monchaux teaches at the Slade School of Fine Art, London. She exhibits regularly, particularly in Paris, and early in 1996 had a one person exhibition at the Sean Kelly Gallery in New York. She had a major solo exhibition at the Whitechapel Gallery, London, in 1997 and has new exhibitions in New York in 1998-99.

David Nash

David Nash was born in Esher, Surrey, in 1945. He studied at Kingston College of Art (1963-64), Brighton College of Art (1964-67) and Chelsea School of Art (1969-70).

In 1970 he moved to Blaenau Ffestiniog where he lives and works; in that year he made his first wooden tower, since destroyed by a gale.

Nash works entirely in wood - wood that no longer has a useful life - and with living plants. Most of his museum exhibitions have been made in wood which was found in the locality of the host museums, ensuring a relevance which is unique and which neatly sidesteps the notion of being site specific in the traditional sense.

David Nash has worked regularly abroad, particularly in Japan, and enjoys considerable international acclaim, with work represented in numerous collections throughout the world.

Two major books were published on David Nash in 1996, *The Sculpture of David Nash*, Julian Andrews, The Henry Moore Foundation and Lund Humpries, and *David Nash, Forms into Time*, with an essay by Marina Warner, Academy Editions.

Paul Neagu

Paul Neagu was born in Bucharest, Romania, in 1938. He studied at the Institute 'N Grigorescu' (1959-65). In 1969 he came to Britain at the invitation of Richard Demarco, and has since lived and worked in London, as a lecturer in fine art, in addition to pursuing his own career as an artist. Neagu gained British citizenship in 1977.

Paul Neagu's sculpture conveys the notion of movement through abstract form. His drawings, paintings, performances and sculpture are closely linked, in that all explore ideas that cannot be made literal in any concrete sense. They invite participation, which is demanding of the viewer's concentration, and need time as well as space to work their way into our consciousness. Star forms and geometric shapes, often made in stainless steel, with the surface worked to textures that capture and refract light, are typical of Neagu's genre.

Eilís O'Connell

Eilís O'Connell was born in Derry, Northern Ireland, in 1953. She studied at Crawford School of Art, Cork (1970-74), Massachusetts College of Art, Boston (1974-75) and again at Crawford School of Art (1975-77). Two fellowships followed: the Arts Council of Northern Ireland British School at Rome Fellowship (1983-84) and the Arts Council PS1 (New York) Fellowship (1987-88).

A distinctive sense of place that Eilís O'Connell manifests in her work may possibly have led her towards undertaking many important public commissions, mostly in urban settings. These include *Secret Station* 1991, for Cardiff Bay Art Trust at the Eastern Gateway, Cardiff, and *The Space Between* 1992, commissioned by the Milton Keynes Development Corporation. During 1994 and 1995 Eilís O'Connell worked on the design for a lifting footbridge in collaboration with Ove Arup for the River Frome at Narrow Quay in central Bristol.

O'Connell's ability to ensure a successful interaction between the object and its environment may well be rooted in her experience of the Irish landscape in which she grew up. *Secret Station*, however, referred to her experience of the British industrial landscape. Her use of steam in this piece, which was pumped out through fissures in large conical forms, a device she first used in 1990, demonstrates her response to factory chimneys and other industrial outlets.

Eilís O'Connell is particularly concerned with the notions of space within objects, spaces between them and, in turn, their spatial relationship to their place. Materials and processes are also carefully chosen, both for their appropriateness and to convey contrast or emphasis.

William Pye

William Pye was born in London in 1938. He studied at Wimbledon School of Art (1958-61) and at the Sculpture School of the Royal College of Art (1961-65). Pye's early and sustained interest in harnessing the largely unpredictable element of water for his sculptures was fuelled by his play and observations as a child. Most of his childhood holidays and weekends were spent near Cutmill Ponds in Surrey, a national beauty spot where the young Pye learnt to swim, playing for hours in a nearby stream. By the age of seventeen he had made his first waterfall.

His sculptures of the 1960s were abstract forms and showed Pye's preference for the traditional materials of metal and stone. Highly polished abstract and geometrical works in stainless steel of the 1970s, some of which were kinetic, became synonymous with his name. Movement, reflection and the use of light in these works led him logically to considering water as an essential part of his artistic expression. The natural world which he explores in his sculptures is interpreted through water and metal, where disarmingly simple concepts become objects of utmost sophistication and great beauty.

William Pye has undertaken many major commissions in the last fifteen years, including the well-known *Slip Stream* and *Jet Stream* water sculptures at Gatwick Airport's North Terminal (1987); a 13 by 70 metres water wall and 'portico' which formed the entrance feature to the British Pavilion at *Expo '92* in Seville (1992); *Tetra Trellis*, a tetrahedron-shaped stainless steel water sculpture at Tetra Pak UK Headquarters, Stockley Park, Middlesex (1993) and *Derby Cascade* in Market Square, Derby (1995). Numerous exhibitions of William Pye's sculptures have been held in Britain and abroad since his first solo exhibition at the Redfern Gallery, London, in 1966. He has also been the recipient of many awards, and in 1993 was elected Honorary Fellow of the Royal Institute of British Architects.

Victoria Rance

Victoria Rance was born in Streatley, Berkshire, in 1959. She studied at North Oxfordshire Technical College (1978-79) and in the Department of Fine Art at the University of Newcastle (1979-83).

On leaving university Victoria Rance spent a year sculpting in Mexico, first in Tepotzlan and then in Erongaricuaro. The experience of working within another culture was enriching in many ways. She found that not only were the churches in a predominantly Catholic country full of elaborate carvings which she enjoyed, but there were other layers within the culture to be explored - Aztec and Mayan art in particular. She also discovered that there was a particular harmony between the people and their art. Being allowed such close participation has left a lasting impression. On her return to Britain Rance worked at studios in Rottingdean before moving to London and then to Greenwich, where she works today. In addition to making her sculpture she teaches English to refugees in Lewisham for two mornings a week, finding that contact with them enriches her life.

In her sculpture Victoria Rance has always been a fabricator rather than a modeller or carver, although she has on occasions worked with clay and with plaster. Her works evolve slowly, but at this time she feels that she is returning to ideas pursued as a student. She has a love of Gabo and the constructivists, and whilst not emulating their work, her acknowledgement may be seen in subtleties of making, in tone and in form. It is the spirituality in her work which leads Rance to look back to historical examples for inspiration - not to works of art, but to objects found in museums and in churches.

Victoria Rance has exhibited her work regularly in group shows in Britain, with solo exhibitions in the late eighties and late nineties. She also works to commission.

Andrew Sabin

Andrew Sabin was born in London in 1958. He studied sculpture at Chelsea College of Art (1979-83).

In the years since graduating, Andrew Sabin has exhibited extensively in Britain and in Europe, including Lausanne, Basel, Lisbon, Rome and Berne. Recent exhibitions at the CREDAC d'Ivry in Paris, the Serpentine Gallery, London, La Fondation Suisse and Le Corbusier in Paris, and at the Henry Moore Institute's studios at Dean Clough, Halifax, led to a point in his career where he began to move away from interior installations towards making sculptures for outdoor locations.

At Dean Clough Andrew Sabin made a massive installation in steel mash and scaffolding of platforms and walk-ways from which the viewer could easily survey the whole studio space. As the supports and enclosures were very open, the sense of being suspended in air imbued the visitor with feelings of insecurity and of weightlessness, adding confusion of balance and perception. Amongst the interconnecting spaces, Sabin wove freer forms which contrasted with the rectilinear grid, creating a complex space of external beauty and encouraging internal contemplation.

Formal elements of this installation emerged in Andrew Sabin's C-Bin project. A prototype C-Bin, a large open container constructed of galvanised steel strips welded to an open mesh, high enough for people to have to throw things inside was installed on the beach at Selsey to receive all kinds of flotsam and jetsam washed up by the sea. Sabin's plan was to position such bins on different beaches around Britain and record the sculptures when the bins were full - sculptures made different by virtue of their contents. Andrew Sabin is now working on another bin project at base camps on Mount Everest, where rubbish accumulates and cannot degrade rapidly because of the low temperatures.

Keir Smith

Keir Smith was born in Kent in 1950. He studied fine art at the University of Newcastle upon Tyne (1969-73) and at Chelsea School of Art (1973-75). His academic interest in art of the Renaissance - painting, sculpture and architecture - is long established, but has emerged only gradually as a presence in his drawing and sculpture.

Working without an agent or dealer, Smith made his way as an artist through public commissions in the 1980s when sculpture trails and the desire for site specific sculpture prevailed. He was appointed artist in residence at Grizedale Forest, Cumbria in 1979 and made a number of publicly sited sculptures including *Towards the Open Sea* for South Hill Park in Bracknell and *Dendron* for Yorkshire Sculpture Park, both in 1983. Smith excelled in his response to such commissions, and in finding an apposite solution which referred to the history of the site and its physical nature, as with *The Iron Road* 1986 for the Forest of Dean where carved wooden railway sleepers lie in the place of a disused track, bearing references to former lives and times particular to the forest. His most recent commission is a work for Henrietta House in the West End of London. Here a sculptural frieze depicting fifteen buildings related stylistically, such as Hawksmoor's Pyramid, The Radcliffe Library and Canary Wharf, to mention only three, flows with and is relevant to the architecture. In addition to the commissions, Keir Smith has exhibited his work regularly in Britain in both solo and group shows. Particularly important was *Flint Sepulchre* at the University of Warwick in 1994.

Drawing serves Keir Smith's sculpture in an indirect way. Long periods are devoted to drawing, not to find solutions for specific sculptures, but to develop ideas. The drawings, in pencil and watercolour, have all the intensity of his sculpture and are no less a result of concentrated activity. Drawings of a different kind fill his sketchbooks and are used in the development of the sculptures.

William Tucker

William Tucker was born in Cairo in 1935, and came to England when his family returned in 1937. He studied history at Oxford University (1955-58) and sculpture at the Central and St Martin's Schools of Art, London (1959-60). Anthony Caro was teaching at St Martin's at the time, and fellow students included David Annesley, Phillip King and Isaac Witkin. Tucker was awarded the Sainsbury Scholarship in 1961 and the Peter Stuyvesant Travel Bursary in 1965. He spent two years as Gregory Fellow at Leeds University Fine Arts Department (1968-70) and represented Britain at the 1972 Venice Biennale.

William Tucker is also a writer, and in 1974 published the *Language of Sculpture* (Thames and Hudson, London) which was released in the United States in 1978 as *Early Modern Sculpture* (Oxford University Press, New York). Following the publication of the book in London he was invited to select *The Condition of Sculpture* exhibition which was held at the Hayward Gallery, London, in 1975, for which he wrote the catalogue essay. Both the book and the exhibition proved to be landmarks in the development of a certain tradition of British sculpture. Tucker moved to New York in 1978 and taught at Colombia University (1978-82) and the New York Studio School. Further fellowships followed: the Guggenheim Fellowship for Sculpture in 1981 and the National Endowment for the Arts Fellowship in 1986, the year he became an American citizen. He is currently co-chair of the Art Programme at Bard College.

Early works, made from steel or wood, were assembled and altered into abstract configurations in largely geometric form. Such compositions were later cast in plaster or concrete, and concerns for weight and gravity and the defiance of those states became important. His exhibition at the Tate Gallery in 1987 and a retrospective at the Storm King Art Centre in 1988 consolidated his reputation in America, with works being acquired by the three major New York museums.

Jim Unsworth

Jim Unsworth was born in Wigan, Lancashire, in 1958. He studied at Reading University (1976-80). The fine art course at Reading was mostly devoted to painting, although Unsworth began to make sculpture whilst he was there. His father had been a coffin-maker and it was a revelation to Unsworth, with his inherited sense of practicality and of craftsmanship, that you could actually make things *and* be an artist.

On leaving college Unsworth worked in a studio in Greenwich among artists who gained a reputation for making welded steel sculptures. He stayed there for fourteen years. The professional contact with other artists was important to him through those years, and work from that time was exhibited in *Kunst Europa* at the Kunstverein in Kirchzarten, Freiburg, part of a nation-wide exhibition of European Artists in Germany in 1991, which was a formative experience for Unsworth.

In 1994 he moved to a studio in Bow with the artists Iain Edwards and Philip Medley. The change of location was mirrored by a significant change in his work, which he contributes partly to time spent carving in Cyprus in 1991 and also to the larger space in which he was working. Large abstract sculptures gave way to figurative works on the theme of the circus. A strong narrative element became important, and the form of the elephant in particular took precedence, not only in large welded steel sculptures but in smaller modelled versions cast in bronze.

Jim Unsworth is reluctant to cite specific influences, but he is very interested in the work of David Smith and of Calder, particularly the latter's circus sculptures.

Unsworth's work can be found in many public collections in Britain. He exhibits frequently in group shows, and has had a significant number of solo exhibitions.

Glynn Williams

Glynn Williams was born in Shrewsbury in 1939. He studied at Wolverhampton College of Art (1955-61). On graduating he won a Rome Scholarship for sculpture, and until 1963 lived and worked at the British School in Rome. After his return to England he taught at a number of art colleges including Leeds. In 1976 he was appointed to run the Sculpture Department at Wimbledon School of Art, setting himself the objective of building a department with clear aims and attitudes towards sculpture.

His first solo exhibition was held at the ICA in London in 1967, since when he has exhibited regularly in Britain and occasionally abroad.

Williams is a leading sculptor of the figurative tradition. Strong and solid forms based on the human figure, sliced and altered, have recently taken over from his more naturalistic sculpture. Some have been coloured or treated in ways that render surfaces more ambiguous.

Glynn Williams is currently Professor of Sculpture at the Royal College of Art, London.

Bill Woodrow

Bill Woodrow was born in Henley-on-Thames in 1948. He studied at Winchester College of Art (1967-68), St Martin's School of Art, London (1968-71) and Chelsea School of Art, London (1971-72). On graduating he showed work in a mixed exhibition at the Museum of Modern Art in Oxford and had his first one-man show at the Whitechapel Art Gallery, London, in 1972. There followed a period of around seven years when circumstances dictated that Woodrow made very little sculpture - he taught at an Inner London comprehensive school, and then full-time on a foundation course in Essex up to 1980. He would make work occasionally, but when in 1978 he got a studio he began to make sculpture on a regular basis.

Woodrow's early sculpture was made from materials found in dumps, used car lots and scrap yards, whether he was working in Britain or abroad. Large, disused consumer goods were the vehicle for his ideas - fridges, motorcar parts, doors, bricks and armchairs altered and placed in new relationships, formed metaphors for all kinds of tales. His 'archaeological' delving into modern detritus and the consequent narrative that he makes is aptly summed up in an essay by William Feaver (*The British Show* catalogue, Art Gallery of New South Wales/The British Council, 1985): 'Ransacking the debris of present-day civilisation, Bill Woodrow fabricates comparable apparitions. His sculpture is proverbial, fabulous. Cherishing the outlandish, rejoicing in the jump cut and the shock decision, he makes dry bones live.'

Collecting as he did, and using all manner of unrelated objects in new configurations, allowed Bill Woodrow to tell stories in his sculpture, and when he began to fabricate pieces in new material in the late 1980s, the narrative element remained. Recent works, cast in bronze, still evoke their eclectic origins, and the story told is equally elusive.

Sculpture at Goodwood

Sculpture at Goodwood is dedicated to commissioning, exhibiting and promoting British contemporary sculpture nationally and internationally. It is a charitable foundation established in 1994 by Wilfred and Jeannette Cass and endowed by them.

Between fifteen and twenty sculptures are enabled annually through a system which covers the casting or fabrication costs of new work and which encourages artists to realise sculptures that may otherwise be beyond their financial reach. The foundation gives artists full support in marketing their work world-wide through the Internet, through Sculpture at Goodwood's annual publications, its outreach programme and through dedicated publicity. When a sculpture is sold the foundation receives back its financial outlay, the major proceeds going to the artist. Sculpture at Goodwood works in close collaboration with artists, with their dealers and with their agents to achieve maximum impact in the market place.

Sculpture at Goodwood is the open-air venue where collectors and the public alike can view contemporary British sculptures in peace and tranquillity. Twenty acres of woodland walks and glades in an area of outstanding natural beauty provide an idyllic setting for he changing display. Goodwood is fifty miles south of London overlooking the Roman city of Chichester and the south coast. It is open to the public from March to November on Thursday, Friday and Saturday between 10.30 am and 4.30 pm.

'...the finest sculpture park in the land'
Antony Thorncroft, Financial Times

'Confident steps into pastoral perspective'
Isabel Carlisle, The Times

Directions to Sculpture at Goodwood

Travelling by car from London

Take the A3 towards Guildford/Portsmouth. Do not leave the A3 at Guildford, but continue past the city and the exits for Farnham and Eashing until you see signs for Milford, Petworth and Haslemere where you leave the motorway. Follow the sign for Petworth and Witley, at the roundabout, passing a left turning to another roundabout where you will join the A283, still in the direction of Petworth and Witley. Pass through Witley, Chiddingfold and Northchapel. On reaching Petworth follow signs for the A272 to Midhurst. Leaving Petworth, follow signs for the A285 to Chichester.You will pass through the village of Duncton and the hamlet of Upwaltham. At the top of the hill coming out of Upwaltham look for a brown signpost indicating a right turning for Goodwood Racecourse and Open Air Museum. Turn right here and follow the road for two miles to a small crossroads, just before the road curves to the left. Turn left between the two lodges and follow the sign to Goodwood House. Sculpture at Goodwood is one mile down this road on the left. Please ring the bell at the gates for entry to the grounds.

Travelling by train from London

Take the Portsmouth Harbour/Bognor Regis train from Victoria Station to Barnham. Trains leave every hour at a few minutes past the hour. The journey time is an hour and forty minutes. Barnham station to Sculpture at Goodwood takes ten minutes by taxi. Please ring the bell at the gates for entry to the grounds.

Travelling by car from Brighton

Take the A27 towards Chichester. At the Tangmere roundabout follow signs for Boxgrove (do not follow signs for Goodwood). Carry on through Boxgrove to a stop sign at a four way intersection. Cross the intersection and continue to a T-junction opposite gates to Goodwood House. Turn right. Sculpture at Goodwood is on the right at the top of the hill. Please ring the bell at the gates for entry to the grounds.

The House and Beginnings

The house at Sculpture at Goodwood was built in 1976/77 by Charles Kearley for his fine collection of twentieth-century art which he left, on his death in1989, to Pallant House in Chichester. Designed in close consultation with local architects, John and Heather Lomax of Hughes, Lomax and Adutt, the design adheres to the Bauhaus principles of repeated cubes and lacks the traditional interior finishes of plaster, skirting, architraves and cornices. Its position in the site is discreet, but with wonderful views through the woodland to Chichester and the coast.

Wilfred and Jeannette Cass bought the house from Kearley's estate in 1989, and having made minor modifications, began to move in during March 1990. Inspired by the views over distant pastures to Chichester Cathedral and the way that their own collection of sculpture was seen to advantage in the grounds, they set about creating Sculpture at Goodwood. The idea of ceasing to build a collection and devote their resources to establishing a charitable foundation to help British sculptors was soon put to work. Their research took them world-wide to many venues which show sculpture in the open air, and through their observations, critical and business-based approach, their plan for Goodwood evolved.

Sculpture at Goodwood now commissions around fifteen or more sculptures a year which it owns in partnership with the sculptors until the time they are sold. At the point of sale the foundation receives back its financial input and a small percentage of the selling price to cover overheads, and the money is ploughed back into new pieces. Goodwood provides continuing support and promotion for British contemporary sculpture. A self-imposed limit of some forty pieces, placed with care in the grounds, ensures uncrowded siting and the opportunity for a unique aesthetic experience.

The Woodland Setting

In the early years much of the copse was overgrown with vines of old man's beard, and many trees had fallen in the devastating storms of 1987 and 1990. When the damaged trees and vines were cleared and spaces created for sculptures, the growth of many species of wild flowers was stimulated by light which had been excluded. Encouraged by this discovery and the success of their first season of planting, the Casses, under the guidance of landscape designer Victor Shanley, forestry engineer Peter Harland and grounds manager Martin Russell, have devised an ongoing plan of woodland renewal. Native species of broad-leaf trees replace conifers and diseased trees, adding to the diversity of stock and providing background colours that change with the seasons whilst changing visitors' experience of the sculptures.

The eastern portion of the copse has been leased at a peppercorn rent to Sculpture at Goodwood by the Duke of Richmond and Gordon, and only since 1993 has it been worked and planted. This area has provided some of the larger sweeps of lawn and long vistas over arable land to the south and north-east.

The twenty-acre site is enclosed on two sides by portions of an historic, listed flint wall which, throughout the Richmond estate, extends for seventeen miles. This was built around 1812 by French prisoners of war who were imprisoned in Portsmouth. They mined the flints locally, and some pits remain as grassed or overgrown hollows in the grounds of Sculpture at Goodwood, one of which forms the open air theatre. A small part of the wall shows the work of a master craftsman, where the napped flints are perfectly cut and mortared, whilst the effort of less skilled artisans bears a more random assembly.

The Sculpture at Goodwood Website
Bringing British sculptors and their work to an international audience

Sculpture at Goodwood's Website has been devised and implemented by Dr Christopher Thorpe. Documentation about Sculpture at Goodwood on the site is historically based on Sculpture at Goodwood books, Information and Education packs. Daily and monthly changes in the displays are recorded and placed on the site as they happen. Each month an artist is featured on the website, with a slideshow of past works, and details of their new comission for Goodwood. Broadcasts of Sculpture at Goodwood's study days, including film, sound recordings and still images, are made on the day of the event. Written material and images of new scuptures are published on the website as they are installed at Goodwood and form the pages for future volumes in this series of books. Artists working at Goodwood, and manufacturing processes such as casting, fabrication, carving and construction are also being featured as the website becomes our prime educational tool, and repository for this unique collection of information and imagery.

We are now producing time-lapse films of the sculptures being installed at Goodwood, so that the process of construction and installation may be recorded for posterity. These unique time-lapse films compress a two or three day installation into between 10 and 20 seconds, and provide a remarkably compelling insight into the difficulties and the intricacies of installing sculpture on such a large scale in an open air setting. These films are akin to all of the video recorded at Goodwood.

The Internet site is only part of Goodwood's cross-media scheme to promote British sculpture, to inform, to record and to educate. Sculpture at Goodwood CD-ROM and DVD packages may be found on pages 135 and 136.

Digital Library, Videos and Audio Tapes

Sculpture at Goodwood has so far established a store of around 10,000 images of contemporary British sculpture and design on Digital Disks which are easy to browse and may be viewed by arrangement in the gallery. The digital library is updated constantly together with the reference library of specialist books, videos and audio tapes on the work of Sculpture at Goodwood and its artists.

Each digital disk holds around one hundred images, and the collection includes the work of Ivor Abrahams, Jane Ackroyd, Edward Allington, John Atkin, Paul Atterbury, Walter Bailey, Zadok Ben-David, Hamish Black, Richard Bray, Peter Burke, Anthony Caro, Nicola Cass, Lynn Chadwick, Ann Christopher, Robin Connelly, Angela Conner, Stephen Cox, Tony Cragg, George Cutts, Andrew Darke, Richard Deacon, John Edwards, Nigel Ellis, John Farnham, Laura Ford, Elisabeth Frink, Steve Geliot, John Gibbons, Bruce Gernand, Andy Goldsworthy, Steven Gregory, Charles Hadcock, Nigel Hall, Nicola Hicks, Shirazeh Houshiary, Jon Isherwood, Allen Jones, Anish Kapoor, Michael Kenny, Phillip King, Bryan Kneale, Langlands and Bell, Stephen Lewis, Tim Lewis, Lilian Lijn, Kim Lim, Peter Logan, Michael Lyons, David Mach, Sally Matthews, Charlotte Mayer, Dhruva Mistry, Cathy de Monchaux, Elizabeth de Monchaux, Nicholas Moreton, Joanna Mowbray, David Nash, Paul Neagu, Colin Nicholas, Eilís O'Connell, Rob Olins, Julian Opie, Ana Maria Pacheco, Cornelia Parker, Trupti Patel, Vong Phaophanit, Charles Poulsen, William Pye, Ronald Rae, Peter Randall-Page, Jim Rattenbury, Paul Roberts-Holmes, Colin Rose, Sophie Ryder, Keir Smith, Susan Stockwell, Michael Sandle, Wendy Taylor, Almuth Tebbenhoff, Simon Thomas, Tim Threlfall, William Tucker, William Turnbull, Roderick Tye, Sheila Vollmer, Richard Wentworth, Glynn Williams, Avril Wilson, Bill Woodrow.

Library and Commissioning Archive

As Sculpture at Goodwood commissions between fifteen and eighteen new sculptures a year, a considerable archive is being built as a result. Artists donate past catalogues and new publications on their work to the library, which adds to the wealth of material assembled by Wilfred and Jeannette Cass since1992 when they founded the charity.

The commissioning process is well recorded, and documentation relating to the production of sculptures and all installation at Goodwood is held on file. In the first four years this amounts to records of some ninety-one sculptures. Records contain visual as well as written and statistical information, and tell the story of how the sculpture commission came about, its realisation, installation and anything else that may occur during these processes. Some are straight forward, others contain complex instructions for footings and installation, crane requirements, logistics for moving and transporting the sculpture, conservation matters, care, recipes for treating wood and finally details relating to sales and loans.

Books and catalogues on British sculptors sit with volumes on other artists. Books on sculpture parks and gardens throughout the world reflect the many travels undertaken by the founders when they were planning Sculpture at Goodwood, and many prove to be irreplaceable as they are now out of print. There are also volumes on other art forms, garden management, historical art and reference works.

The fact that this library is being built in parallel with the digital library, CD-ROMs, DVD and the Internet site makes Sculpture at Goodwood a centre of information on British sculpture.

Publications

British Contemporary Sculpture at Goodwood 95/96 £30
British Contemporary Sculpture at Goodwood 96/97 £10
British Contemporary Sculpture at Goodwood 97/98 £10
British Contemporary Sculpture at Goodwood 98/99 £10

Sculpture at Goodwood books are published annually and form a history of commissions leading to an overview of British sculpture as seen through the works displayed at Goodwood. The first volume was published in 1995.

Drawings and Models Sculpture at Goodwood 94/98 £5
CD Rom version £30

The first book and CD-ROM cataloguing drawings and models from Sculpture at Goodwood.

Introducing Sculpture at Goodwood Video £5

The Sculpture at Goodwood video features the opening of the foundation in 1994, and is a short introduction to its sculptures and intentions.

Open College of the Arts Educational Package £40
The package contains a video with extensive footage on Sculpture at Goodwood, written information and guidelines on looking at sculpture.

Designers

The work of young designers, most of whom are under the age of twenty-five, is an important aspect of Sculpture at Goodwood. From the time they established the foundation, Wilfred and Jeannette Cass have sought out innovative seating, signing and buildings for the grounds, as well as furniture for the gallery and office. Pieces which demonstrate an inventive use of materials and form are commissioned to show a range of design and making processes. Their display in the grounds is functional and devised to encourage others to support the work of these young artists..

Items by Ben Brooks, Alison Crowther, John Greed, Thomas Heatherwick, David Harvey, James Paget, Jim Partridge, Johnny Woodford and students of Hooke Park College in the form of desks, seats and shelters has been commissioned. Materials used include various native and tropical hard woods, carbon fibre, glass, perspex, green wood, metals, stones and cements. Looking to the future, we hope to add more, and to include recycled materials.

Inspirations for seating range from water (Ben Brooks) through all kinds of organic forms (Alison Crowther, James Paget, Johnny Woodford) to mathematical devices worked out with the assistance of a computer (Thomas Heatherwick). Techniques demonstrated in the collection range through casting, laminating, moulding, carving, welding and construction. Information about these works together with the addresses and telephone numbers of the designers is available for visitors in the gallery. Most pieces were illustrated in the second volume in this series, Sculpture at Goodwood 96/97.

Sculptors' Drawings and Models

Since 1994 Sculpture at Goodwood has collected sculptors' drawings and models which are related to new sculptures from British artists. The drawings now number almost sixty, and are startling in their scale and in the range of mediums artists have used. Differing approaches to making drawings are evident in the collection; some are original plans of a technical nature, some are visions, others, such as Anthony Caro's life drawing, are parallel expressions of form and volume. Some are reflections about the sculpture made after it was made and installed at Sculpture at Goodwood. Some drawings are as monumental as the sculptures they represent. One charcoal drawing by Peter Randall-Page, an impression of a sculpture before it was made, measures 200 x 300 cm. *Endeavour: Cannon Dredged from the First Wreck of the Ship of Fools* by Bill Woodrow is close in size. Intricate drawings by Allen Jones of his visions for *Temple* and Shirazeh Houshiary's technical specifications for *The Extended Shadow* show different ways of working on ideas for sculptures. *Space Emptied Out* by Eilis O'Connell shows her sculpture as it appeared in the glade at Sculpture at Goodwood. An abstract, mixed- media colour composition by Phillip King expresses balance and dynamic movement without revealing literal structure. Each drawing has a unique relationship with its sculpture.

The drawings and models now form an exhibition which is offered on loan by Sculpture at Goodwood to galleries which conform to international curatorial guidelines for the safe exhibition of works on paper. A stable, secure environment is required: light levels should be no more than 50 Lux and relative humidity at around 33%. Interested galleries should contact Sculpture at Goodwood to receive further information and a catalogue and CD-ROM.

Sculptures 1994-98

with page numbers for the sculptures illustrated in this volume

Edward Allington *Fallen Pediment (Piano)* 1994 [p90]
Kenneth Armitage *Richmond Oak* 1985-90

Zadok Ben-David *Conversation Piece* 1996 [p64]

Hamish Black *YP 1* 1998 [p82]

Matt Bodimeade *Force 7* 1990

Peter Burke *Host* 1996 [p74]

Sir Anthony Caro *The Tower of Discovery* 1991

Sir Anthony Caro *Goodwood Steps (Spirals)* 1994-96 [p14]

Lynn Chadwick *Stranger III* 1959 (cast 1996) [p26]

Robin Connelly Oak *Spiral* 1991

Stephen Cox *Organs of Action - speeech, evacuation, procreation, grasp, gait* 1987-88

Stephen Cox *Granite Catamarans on a Granite Wave* 1994 [p68]

Tony Cragg *Spill* 1987 [p36]

Tony Cragg *Trilobites* 1989

Tony Cragg *Pillars of Salt* 1998 [p56]

Maggie Cullen *Untitled I* 1997 [p34]

George Cutts *The Kiss* 1991

George Cutts *Sea Change* 1996

Grenville Davey *Button* 1988

John Davies *Head* 1997 [p32]

Richard Deacon *When the Landmasses First Appeared* 1986

Eva Drewett *Around Man* 1991

Eva Drewett *The Human Side of Being II* 1992

Iain Edwards *Reinventing the Wheel* 1998 [p22]

Nigel Ellis *Mindfulness of Breathing* 1998 [p16]

Ian Hamilton Finlay *The World Has Been Empty Since the Romans* 1985 [p24]

Laura Ford *Nature Girls* 1996

Elisabeth Frink *Horse and Rider* 1969

Elisabeth Frink *Riace Figures I, II, III, IV* 1986, 1987,1988, 1989

William Furlong *Walls of Sound* 1998 [p44]

Bruce Gernand *Hearts-Hide* 1993

Andy Goldsworthy *Herd of Arches* 1994 [p40]

Andy Goldsworthy *A Clearing of Arches. For the Night* 1995

Steven Gregory *Bag Men* 1993

Steven Gregory *Paparazzi* 1996 [

Steven Gregory *Fish on a Bicycle* 1998 [p50]

Steven Gregory The *Two of Us* 1998 [p18]

Charles Hadcock *Caesura IV* 1995 [p48]

Nigel Hall *Soglio (Goodwood)* 1994 [p88]

Nicola Hicks *Recovered Memory* 1996-97 [p 38]

Shirazeh Houshiary *The Extended Shadow* 1994

Allen Jones *Temple* 1998 [p80]

Michael Kenny *In Secrecy and Solitude* 1991-92

Michael Kenny *Belief and Desire* 1997-98 [p86]

Phillip King *Genghis Khan* 1963

Phillip King *Slant* 1966

Phillip King *Academy Piece* 1971

Bryan Kneale *Deemster Fish* 1996 [p86]

Langlands and Bell *Fifty Cities* 1997

Kim Lim *Spiral II* 1983

Peter Logan *Duet for Two Flutes* 1991

Richard Long *Six Stone Circles* 1981

Michael Lyons *Amphitrite* 1993

David Mach *The Garden Urn* 1996 [p42]

David Mach *The Wild Bunch!* 1996

John Maine *Enclosure* 1995

Bernard Meadows *Large Seated Armed Figure* 1963

Dhruva Mistry *The Object* 1995-97 [p28]

Cathy De Monchaux *Confessional* 1997-98 [p58]

David Nash *Charred Column* 1993

David Nash *Two Together* 1994

David Nash *Mosaic Eggs* 1995

David Nash *Large Oak Throne etc* 1997 [p76]

Paul Neagu *Triple Star Head* 1987-93

Paul Neagu *Unnamed (Eschaton)* 1997 [p84]

Eilis O'Connell *Space Emptied Out* 1994 [p78]

Ana Maria Pacheco *Requiem* 1986-95

Trupti Patel *Stay* 1995

Vong Phaophanit *Azure Neon Body* 1994-95

William Pye *Vessel III* 1995

William Pye *Miss Prism* 1998 [p54]

Victoria Rance *Ark* 1997 [p60]

Peter Randall-Page *Ways to Wrap a Stone I* 1990

Peter Randall-Page *Ways to Wrap a Stone II* 1990

Peter Randall-Page *Beneath the Skin* 1991

Peter Randall-Page *Secret Life I & IV* 1994

Colin Rose *Breeze* 1991

Colin Rose *Night and Day* 1992

Sophie Ryder *The Boxing Hares* 1988

Andrew Sabin *Land-Bin* 1998 [p66]

Michael Sandle *A Mighty Blow for Freedom: Fuck the Media* 1988

Keir Smith *Stefano* 1997 [p30]

William Tucker *Frenhofer* 1997 [p70]

William Turnbull *Large Spade Venus* 1986

William Turnbull *Gate* 1972

Jim Unsworth *Another Surprise for Fabricius Luscinus* 1998 [p46]

Glynn Williams *Portrait with Flowers* 1990-91

Glynn Williams *Gateway of Hands* 1992 [p20]

Avril Wilson *A Leaf with Halo* 1991

Bill Woodrow *Endeavour: Cannon Dredged from the First Wreck of the Ship of Fools* 1994 [p52]

Bill Woodrow *Sitting on History I* 1990-95 [p72]

Models and Maquettes

Hamish Black
Model for *YP1* 1997
Yellow Pages directory, rolled and cut

Peter Burke
Maquette for Host 1996
lead

Nigel Ellis
Maquette for *Mindfulness of Breathing* 1998
plaster

Steven Gregory
Maquette for *The Two of Us* 1998
bronze

Charles Hadcock
Maquette for *Caesura IV* 1995
bronze

Bryan Kneale
Model for *Deemster Fish* 1996
steel

Langlands and Bell
Model for *Fifty Cities* 1997
core foam

Dhruva Mistry
Model for *'The Object'* 1995
card

Keir Smith
Model for *Stefano* 1996
wood, flint painted

William Tucker
Maquette for *Frenhofer* 1994
bronze

Acknowledgements

Jane Allison
Robert Allison
Ian Barker
Roger Bamber
David Barrie
Mary-Rose Beaumont
Sarah Bishop
David Booth
Dennis Burgess
Sir Anthony Caro
Mark & Dana Cass
Eric & Jean Cass
Jan Chalmers
David Cohen
Gill Coope
Bronny Cunningham
John Dewey
Jill Dickens
Sir Philip Dowson
Nigel Draffan
Peter Eade
Leighton Evans
Biddy Elkins
Hilary Escolme
Rod Fabricius
Angela & Matthew Flowers
Sir Norman Foster
Sue Freeborough
Martin Friedman
Helen Friend
Fred Goddard
Carol Godsmark
David Gordon
Ben Gottesman
David Gronow
Geraldine Hamilton
Peter Harland
Gill Hedley
Phil Henty
Angus & Anne Hewat
Ros Hitchens
Robert Hopper
Image Bank
Will Jenkins
Anne Jeffries
Annely Juda
Janet Kahn
Derek Kartun
James Kelly
David Laker
Judy Lane
Stuart Le Fevre
Prue Leith
Tim Llewellyn
Nicholas Logsdail
Annette Lovell
Norbert Lynton
The Earl & Countess of March
Tim Marlow
Vicki Meddows-Smith
Brian Miles
Peter Mimpress
Richard E Mitchell
David Mitchinson
Amanda Moses
Peter Murray
Frank Naylor
Corinne Older
David Parfitt
Sir Michael Peat
Gillian Peters
Mr & Mrs Maurice Pinto
Caroline Read
The Duke of Richmond
John Rowan
Martin Russell
Tim Sandys-Renton
Nicholas Serota
Victor Shanley
Neil Shave
Jane Smith
Roffe Swayne
Eleanor Thomas
Elizabeth Thomson
Christopher Thorpe
Jean Thorpe
Peter Thorpe
Stefan van Raay
Jo Walters
Margaret Weld
Jon Whalley
Bill Witcomb
Jonathan Witcomb
Marion Witcomb
Lord Harry Woolf
Gillian Young

Index

Texts
Ann Elliott

Editing
Angela Dyer

Design Consultant
Mervyn Kurlansky

Digital Design
Dr Christopher Thorpe

Photography
Frank Naylor

Printing
Crown Colourprint Limited

ISBN
0 9525233 4 5

Sculpture at Goodwood
Goodwood, West Sussex PO18 0QP
Telephone +44 (0)1243 538449
Fax +44 (0)1243 531853
Directions +44 (0)1243 771114
e-mail w@sculpture.org.uk
Internet www.sculpture.org.uk
reg charity no. 1015088

Open March-November
Thursday, Friday, Saturday 10.30 am - 4.30 pm